Superpower China
Chinese world pow

History, Politics, Education, ┗ ┛ Military

©2020, Hermann Rupold

Publisher: Expertengruppe Verlag

Superpower China – Understanding the Chinese world power from Asia

History, Politics, Education, Economy and Military

Expertengruppe Verlag

CONTENTS

ABOUT THE AUTHOR

Hermann Rupold has been living in Hamburg with his wife, Charlotte, for three years. After being stationed in many places, mainly in Africa, Asia and South America, he eventually found his way to the Elbe to settle down.

Ever since he completed his studies in political science, more than 25 years ago, he has been interested in political, social and historical marginal subjects, which are less well-known but nevertheless widely accepted among scientists. As a teacher, he likes to share his knowledge with his students, but is also able to reach a much wider range of people through his publications.

In his books he concentrates mainly on subjects which not only mean a lot to him personally, but also on the effects such subjects have on the various sections of society, which are less well known. All of his publications are based not only on general scientific research but also encompass his own very personal experiences and knowledge. Every one of his publications, therefore, is based not only on essential scientific principles but also on his very personal experiences and knowledge. In this way his books reflect not only purely factual details but are also practical works which show his broad range of knowledge together with useful tips, which are easy to understand and to follow.

Hermann Rupold's easy to read books put the reader into a relaxed and pleasant ambience, while gaining insight into a subject which few people know much about but most people can profit from.

With this work, he would like to awaken your curiosity towards foreign cultures, break down preconceptions and motivate you to see the big picture.

PREFACE

Before we look closer at the People's Republic of China, we should be aware of one thing: The "Middle Realm" is a country where the contrasts could not be more extreme. Huge mega-cities, which can compete with metropolitan regions, such as New York on the one side, and completely rural regions which hardly produce enough food to sustain existence for the folk, who live in the simplest of huts, on the other. Gigantic motorways as well as traditional rice terraces define the countryside. The ergonomic bicycle helmets of the cyclists in the smog-filled streets are in stark contrast to the conical hats of the farmers in the rural backwaters. Despite all these differences, the economy is booming in the country like in no other national economy.

Many things are possible in China: High-rise buildings, the plans of which are still lying in the architect's office, can be completed in eight days. Internet market salesmen are sending packages to Germany at a cost which seem only just to cover the cost of the packaging. It is not easy for the untrained eye to see how these businesses make their profits. In fact, it is the mass export of goods which has helped the People's Republic to earn the title of "Export World Champion", a title which the Republic of Germany was able to boast about for many years.

China has become the global "winner" in almost all branches of the economy. Food, automotive and digital technology: On all products, the label "Made in China" presents itself proudly. However, the price of the economy boom is high. Even though the description "People's Republic" suggests a profound co-determination of the citizens, everyday life looks very different. The country could be described as a dictatorship, an authoritarian system. Protection of employment, the justice system and social welfare in China cannot be compared to western standards.

That is exactly the reason why everything is different in China. When a hospital needs to be built in a week, then that will happen without regard to work safety or regulation breaks. There is no opposition to complain to about grievances, in the internet there are no free social media platforms where political opinions can be discussed. Still, China has arrived in the present day and is investing everywhere and all the time, whether it be in a dam for the Chinese provinces or the purchase of a complete automotive manufacturer in South Korea. Expansion, fusions or takeovers are all part of the economic plan of this new land of unlimited possibilities.

Comparatively speaking, these possibilities have made China one of the world's biggest economies. In 2017, the country exported goods to the value of almost 2.3 trillion US Dollars. This alarmed not only the international economy but also the politicians. Elected German representatives are already warning that China will have left the European Union behind in ten years.

China seems to be a country of contradictions. In order to understand the economic development, it is not only helpful but also necessary to take a look at this country's history. Several times in its history, China has exerted a great deal of influence on the world but now it is, for the first time, what it always wanted to be: A global superpower. It was a long journey to achieve it, through dozens of wars and just as many reforms. However, it was in the middle of the twentieth century when the country began its triumphant progress, worldwide. But can the People's Republic really keep achieving its success in this form?

- Chapter 1 -

THE HISTORY OF CHINA

TAKING A CLOSER LOOK

Looking at China and its former empires chrono-
logically, they can be divided into five main eras: The
early cultures of the Neolithic period, the early
dynasties, the Imperial Era, the Republic of China and
the People's Republic of China as we know it today. The
following summary gives an insight into the chrono-
logical sequence, from the early cultures of the
present-day Chinese territory up to the establishment
of the People's Republic of China in October, 1949. The
development of the individual dynasties is much more
complicated than I have depicted them. At some points
in history there was temporal overlapping, where at
times the great empire was not unified. Many attempts
were made to unify the region, some with more, some
with less success. Until the formation of the People's
Republic, there had been no long-term stability in
these attempts. Historical documents are patchy, so

the below-mentioned periods are only estimations, although it is possible to divide them up.

Early cultures of the Neolithic period:

~ 7000 – 4000 BC: Hemudu culture

~ 5000 – 2000 BC: Yangshao culture

~ 3000 – 2000 BC: Longshan culture

~ 3300 – 2200 BC: Lianghzu culture

The early dynasties:

~ 2070 – 1600 BC: Xia Dynasty

~ 1700 – 1100 BC: Shang Dynasty

~ 1100 – 256 BC: Zhou Dynasty

The Imperial Era:

~ 221 – 207 BC: Qin Dynasty

~ 206 BC – 220 AD: Han Dynasty

220 – 280 AD: Three kingdoms period

265 – 420 AD: Jin Dynasty

420 – 589 AD: The southern and northern dynasties

581 – 618 AD: Sui Dynasty

618 – 907 AD: Tang Dynasty

907 – 960 AD: The five dynasties and ten kingdoms

960 – 1279 AD: Song Dynasty

1261 – 1368 AD:	Yuan Dynasty
1368 – 1644 AD:	Ming Dynasty
1644 – 1911 AD:	Qing Dynasty

Modern times:

| 1912 – 1949 AD: | Republic of China |
| 1949 – today: | People's Republic of China |

THE EARLY CULTURES

The history of the region that we call today the People's Republic of China is long and eventful. In our history books we find an extremely long list of various dynasties and reigns of various emperors. The existence of heavenly emperors and earthly emperors is documented. However, it is more than questionable whether the events transpired as they are told in the legends. The Middle Realm is full of myths and legends which are ever-present in Chinese everyday life and play a relatively large role.

It is proven that the area of today's China has been populated for at least 40,000 years. Archaeologists are able to make that assumption after the discovery of a fossil, which they called "Tianyuan 1".

Bone fragments of modern humans were found in a cave with the same name, close to Beijing. Taking into consideration the examination of animal bones, found in close proximity, the Tianyuan human was almost certainly a hunter and fisherman who preferred to eat venison and large amounts of freshwater fish. The breakdown of his eating habits was important:

Scientists were able to reconstruct the lives of Homo Sapiens – the modern human – with the assumption that they followed the east Asian rivers when they left the African continent. The reason for the migration along the waterways was their ability to catch fish and therefore would have a relatively easy access to food all year long.

However, the assumption that the hunter from Tianyuan was part of an early human tribe is improbable. China today is made up of various very diverse cultures. This can be proved by the many artifacts which have been found, in the form of receptacles, using a specific form of pottery making technique. Ceramics with the so-called cord-patterned decorations were popular throughout the region. Small differences in manufacture suggest that these artefacts were made by different people.

Archaeologists believe that these works of art were made at a time before the people settled in dwellings. For thousands of years, humans ate wild animals and collected various berries, roots and nuts. In about 6000 BC, humans began tending fields. The remains of settlements along the Yellow River date back to about

5000 BC. At that time, there was a massive change in climate which had a lasting effect on the weather. It became colder and forced the tribes of northern China to migrate to the warmer climate of the south. The tribes from the northern regions showed marked cultural differences to their southern neighbours. This could mostly be seen by the arable crops they farmed. While people from the north were planting millet, those of the south were already farming wet rice, a product in which China is still the world market leader.

Generally, the Chinese cultures had reached a high cultural and technical standard. It was known that they kept pets and that they glazed ceramics. The production of silk was also already an established craft. According to experts, the earliest found silk dates back almost 5300 years. The Erlitou culture of the current province of Henan is particularly worth mentioning in this respect. In addition to their high standard of craftsmanship, the citizens were subject to a high level of administration with strict rules. With that, the foundations were laid for the later dynasties of the Imperial Era and the first hierarchical successions. This modernisation led to the next era in Chinese history.

THE EARLY DYNASTIES

The dynasties of the Chinese emperors are seen as the first stable, regulated succession of rulers in ancient times. However, they were not homogenous dynasties and there were no emperors or kings who were able to rule over all the people at the same time. It is probable that tribes, such as the Xia, Shang and Zhou, were initially independent tribes who decided to combine their interests after expansion of their lands led to conflicting interests between them. Some calculations put this period at around 2000 BC, although this is not by any means sure. There are a lot of chronicles and other documents which have not been found for the Xia Dynasty. There is also no written source to prove that there was a Shang Dynasty.

From a historical point of view, it is significant that Daoism was created during this time. This is a Chinese form of philosophy and a way of looking at the world which had a great influence on the country. In addition to Confucius and Buddhism, Daoism became one of the greatest philosophical developments which influences every part of the lives of Chinese citizens, even today.

During the late Zhou Dynasty there was a great deal of unrest in society leading to political change. A huge explosion in population caused the different kingdoms to merge, the relationship between them became closer. This was of great importance because the country was far from united. 170 individual kingdoms have been recorded from the time of the Zhou Dynasty. However, there was a form of widespread communal identity which was felt during that period. The inhabitants from the various kingdoms did feel themselves to be part of a nation. This way of looking at the world was in deep contrast to the tiny kingdoms in Europe during the Middle Ages, as an example. The kingdoms in China grew closer together despite or because of interactions between families, fighting and commercial interests. In addition, they were going through a phase of modernisation. The Bronze Age was long gone and iron tools and weapons were in common use. There were also ground-breaking intellectual advances in that period. During the last years of the Zhou Dynasty there was a large number of philosophers, dating around 200 BC. The rulers of the Zhou Dynasty kingdoms found themselves losing power, due to the increasing centralisation of its people. In the end, the downfall of the Zhou Dynasty could not be prevented and the Imperial Era, the most characteristic era for the Chinese people, began.

THE IMPERIAL ERA

The reign of the Chinese Emperors lasted nearly 2000 years, an extraordinarily long time. There is hardly a world power in history which has lasted so long. However, this period was not known for its peacefulness or wealth. Inner-political disagreements and permanent raids from the nomadic people afflicted the empire. The latter led to the erection of one of the most distinctive structures in human history, which is steeped in myths and legends: The Chinese Wall. Emperor Qin Shihuandi, one of the best-known potentates in Chinese history, was responsible for building this bulwark against the barbarians from the northern regions, who were constantly attacking them.

The Emperor is said to be responsible for organising the production of the terracotta army. 8000 stone soldiers are said to be protecting Qin Shihuandi's mausoleum, even after his death. This is an unbelievable treasure for historians and archaeologists. The depiction of the soldiers offers a priceless look into the military of this time and one can see that even at that time – about 220 AD – the Empire possessed an army which was well organised and demonstrated great power against those who threatened it. The detailed depiction of weapons, armour and uniforms gives us an impression of the technical advancements achieved within the imperial army.

This makes the army of Qin Shihuandi an important indication of the power of China in the early part of the first millennium. The only army which comes close to that is the legions of the Roman Empire, whose initial strong organisation weakened in Europe over the centuries. It was not until the Middle Ages again when the rulers within central Europe organised themselves standing armies of a comparable size. In addition, the soldiers and generals depicted the excellent technical and artistic skills of that era. Due to the extreme value of the terracotta army, the mausoleum of Qin Shihuandi had not been made available for public viewing. This is not the case with the Great Wall. This fortification is on public view in several places and has become a tourist hot spot and symbol for mass tourism.

It is not only the military and architecture which are of cultural importance. The Imperial Era was known for its technological progress. The Middle Realm was always a step ahead of European culture. Paper and black powder are well-known inventions of the Chinese. In particular, Chinese crafts were revolutionary for their time. In the 4th century, Chinese smiths were able to forge cast iron, leading the way to the eventual development of steel, which was no longer far off. As far back as 6th century, they knew how to harden iron in the far east, using techniques which are still used in the building industry, even today. Even though production of steel originated in China, it still had to be rediscovered in Europe. It took more than 1350 years before a group of German and French experts, advising the inventor Werner von Siemens, to claim the procedure as their own, while the empire in the far east already knew how to use this technique. There are documents to show that in China about 150,000 tons of iron and steel were being produced in about 1100 AD. It was not possible for European countries to produce this amount, even by the beginning of industrialisation in the 18th century.

Blood pressure is another example of forgotten knowledge from China. In 9th century, wood block printing was in brought to Europe and the first prints on ceramic can be dated back to the year 1040. It was only the material which was different in the invention of Johannes Gutenberg from Mainz, Germany, because the technique was already known. Gutenberg's innovation was the use of movable metal letters, which led to a cultural revolution in the late Middle Ages in Europe. The basic technique again in this instance originated in China. In the end, the Gutenberg printing press found its way back to the far east. In 1833, about 800 years after the Chinese began using wooden blocks, Portuguese colonial rulers took back the book printing technique and began to use it in Macau.

Progress in all areas lasted a whole millennium. Between 500 and 1500 AD, Chinese culture was far more advanced than that in Europe in every way. This period is characterised mainly by innovations and inventions. In the natural sciences, too, such as physics, mathematics or astronomy, China was far ahead of Europe. The same applied to agricultural technology. New forms of farming rice guaranteed that the increasing population could be fed. It is said that China had a remarkable 100 million inhabitants by the 12th century. An additional economic upsurge was achieved by the export of porcelain and silk products which were enjoyed by Europeans as luxury goods. As far back as the Middle Ages, China was a powerful force in Asia but, despite that, it was not a Middle Age utopia. Internal fighting was prevalent and there was a great deal of hard and punishing bureaucracy, not to mention the enormous amount of militarisation in the society. There was also discrimination: In South China the inhabitants nurtured a high degree of prejudice against the inhabitants of northern China; they thought themselves to be "more valuable". Despite this disparity, they always considered themselves to be a united nation and they were deeply conscious of their economic, scientific and technological superiority, compared to other state systems. This extreme feeling of self-esteem manifested itself in Sino-centrism, the ideology that China was the cultural centre of the world.

EXCURSUS: CHINA AS THE EMBODIMENT OF ADVANCED CIVILISATION.

Sinocentrism describes an ideology that China had a very special place in the world and that it was the only really civilised country in the world. This ideology was not only considered to be an indisputable fact by China, it also controlled the political landscape throughout southern Asia for two thousand years. The rulers of China acted accordingly: in contact with other nations they acted from the position of the superior party. They thought it was their right to be considered the unrivalled land of progress. They believed themselves to be totally civilised, every other country was considered "barbaric". There was no nuance in their beliefs: Mongolian nomads were thought to no less barbaric than repre-sentatives of the feudal systems during the European late Middle Ages.

The sinocentric ideology remained right up to modern times. In the 18th century, however, other nations started to become serious competitors for China. Painful military defeats also added to the crumbling concept of complete superiority. China did not recognise that it was no longer the centre of the universe until 20th century, although there is still a certain amount of that thought pattern present, even today. The Chinese no longer see themselves as a super-power but they still consider themselves to be special. This can be seen for example in discussions about how much they feel responsible for limiting climate change, or how little. There are other examples of how historical sinocentrism can be seen today, such as in the difficult relationship they have with their neighbours South Korea and Japan. The bitter competition in east Asian can be seen particularly in respect to economic or geopolitical questions.

THE END OF THE IMPERIAL ERA

Sinocentrism reached its peak in the Qing Dynasty. The economic, political and cultural culture promoted by the Qing Emperor was considered to be very successful and characteristic for the whole of China. In the early 19th century, there were others aspiring to be powerful and successful. The surplus which the Chinese were generating on their tea exports to the British Empire resulted in pressure being brought by the British to counter it, thus bringing about an early form of a trade war. The English answered by exporting opium to China, causing enormous problems. Marketing this addictive substance was strictly forbidden in China. The English refused to accept that and continued to deliver the destructive drug unchecked. The English continued their drug-smuggling activities causing great annoyance to the Chinese. When the Chinese authorities seized the drug, this led to the first opium war (1839-1842). Defenceless against the technically superior fleet of the British Empire, China had to admit defeat. England enforced the opium trade with military force until, at some point, the exports began to stagnate and the English blamed the Qing Dynasty for the losses. The English – this time with help from the

French – answered again with military force when in October, 1856, the Chinese authorities demanded to inspect a ship which was flying under the British flag. The Chinese had not been allowed to do that since the first opium war and there was conflict once again. The second opium war lasted for four years and did not end until 1860.

The inhabitants of China suffered greatly, not only through the war itself but also through its after-effects. Due to the prevalent use of opium during that time, millions of people had become addicted to it. After the opium wars, the Chinese government had to make concessions. A prominent example is the relinquishment of Hong Kong to the United Kingdom. Other consequences were the so-called "treaty ports" and "open cities" where the foreign powers could behave with absolute sovereignty. That resulted in China practically being divided up into spheres of interest among the various foreign (commercial) powers. In those areas, the representatives of the foreign nations had absolute power, as they had exercised in other colonies, such as Africa. A good example for this kind of behaviour was the city of Tianjian. Eight European countries gave themselves trade concessions, among them even countries without great colonial histories, such as the Austrian-Hungarian Empire. These concessions were designed to benefit only one side and little consideration was given to the citizens. China became to look more like a foreign colony than an empire. The British exercised their powers most strongly and became the (unofficial) rulers. At the same time as the traders, the Christian missionaries arrived and visibly changed the face of the country. China suffered badly, economically, as a result of the trade deals. Mass poverty and the first uprisings were the result, such as the well-known Boxer Rebellion. Nationalist forces within the Chinese population retaliated against the imperial occupiers of their land. The name "boxer" comes from the west and was so-called because of the traditional martial arts training which the rebels were given. They called themselves the Yihequan, the "fist of justice and harmony". The supposition that they could seriously harm the highly sophisticated opponents with their bare hands or simple weapons was disastrous. Japan, Russia, the United Kingdom, France, the USA, the German Empire, Austria-Hungary and Italy all joined in together to use their modern weapons in the fight. The supporters of the Boxer Movement, on the other hand, chose to use invulnerability rituals and other mythical techniques. A fatal mistake: The Boxers were destroyed by their enemies.

After this disastrous defeat, the Emperor of the ruling Qing Dynasty was under pressure. The necessary reform attempts, demanded by many were blighted by military coups, attempts to modernise destroyed by armed conflicts. The army was practically uncontrollable for the generals. China's soldiers were seen as a prime example of corruption and unreliability. Troops deserted regularly as they did not receive their pay. However, conditions were not only bad in the military sense, they had been ruined by the commercial monopolies of the imperial forces, leaving the population demoralised. This caused the already ailing economy to become even worse. In 1910, pneumonic plague and other natural catastrophes, such as floods, added to the misery. In short: The Qing Dynasty lay in ruins.

This was the ideal breeding ground for opposition movements. In the early 20th century, reformists, wanting a constitutional monarchy, tried to gain power. In addition, revolutionaries aspired to establish the Republic of China.

Again, there were brutal fights in the so-called Xinhai Revolution. 1912 marked the end of the 2100-year old Chinese Imperial Era. The last Emperor, 6-year old Puyi, renounced his throne. The Republic of China was formed, but that did not result in the much-hoped stability of the land.

THE REPUBLIC OF CHINA

The Republic of China was formed by the revolutionary and reformer, Sun Yat-Sen, who formed the Kuonmintang Party a little later in 1912. Sun Yat-Sen assumed a tragic role in the Xinhai Revolution. He organised the revolution, and with it the overthrow of the Imperial Empire from his exile. The Kuonmintang Party was seen as nationalist and won the majority in the National Assembly, enabling them to choose the President of the Republic of China. Sun Yat-Sen was chosen as the first president, but this was only granted on a provisional basis. A constitution, modelled on that of the USA, was ratified. But Sun Yat-Sen could not hold onto power. By early year, Sun Yat-Sen gave up his title to Yuan Shikai, a civil servant and officer. Yuan Shikai was not a man of the people and ruled with an iron hand. He outlawed the Kuonmintang, amended the still young constitution and gave more authority to the military. Yuan Shikai was intensely disliked. In military circles they liked the idea of a republic but did not like the idea of having a dictator. He made many territorial and economic concessions to the arch-enemy Japan, which increased the dislike of his people towards him. He was not deposed: On 6th June 1916, the autocrat died in Beijing. His death resulted once again in the widespread destabilisation of the country. China broke down into countless territories, run by dozens of warlords and ruled by force of arms.

The academic elite of the country searched for solutions to the situation. One social movement sought to form a democratic government, according to western standards. That concept resulted in a social movement: In 1919, after the end of the 1st World War, the victorious armies of the allies, to which China had belonged from 1917 onwards, signed the Treaty of Versailles. In that agreement, the future of the province Shandong was regulated. Shandong was leased to the Germans at the time and, through the treaty, the Chinese assured themselves that it would be given back to them. However, the treaty in fact handed over these rights to Japan. The Chinese government signed the treaty with a great deal of unwillingness. Protests flared up all over the country, resulting in the Movement of 4th May, and causing widespread anti-Japanese and nationalist sentiments.

The foreign powers present in China destabilised the country even further when Japan, the Soviet Union, the USA, France and Great Britain each supported different warlords and generals, providing them with war material. It was good business for the world powers: At one point, China was the country with the worldwide greatest import of arms. These imports were all dealt with the same way: The foreign powers did not define a specific amount of orders and supported various warlords at different times. Fragile alliances were forged and shortly after disbanded. There were no clearly defined lines between friend or foe. Ultimately, it was a question of turnover in weapon sales. That all resulted in four civil wars between 1920 and 1926. The aims of the foreign powers were fulfilled: Both the Soviet Union and Great Britain wanted a weak China which was easy to control.

The threat did not only come from the inner-political unrest. The greatest threat during the 1920s came from Japan and the Soviet Union. The latter took place from 1922 during the rule of Josef Stalin, who was not afraid to involve himself in the inner-political affairs of China. In 1921 the Communist Party of China (CPC) was founded. Stalin strived to make an alliance between the communists and the Kuonmintang. This alliance was called the "First United Front" and Stalin's plan was obvious: The lesser-known CPC, which was still in its infancy should become politically stronger. This was just the beginning of the CPC's success.

The alliance was not only limited to political work, the military forces also began working together. Together, they were very successful in defeating a warlord in northern China. Despite this success, in the end the two parties fell apart, the alliance shattered and then began the longest internal conflict in China's history. Initiated by international communist groups, the "Autumn Harvest Uprising" occurred, followed by the Chinese Civil War.

Despite all resistance, Chiang Kai-shek, the leader of the Kuonmintang, succeeded in uniting the country which had been split for years. In 1928, a united China was formally declared but new conflicts flared up, resulting in a war on four fronts against the Soviet Union, Japan and Great Britain, as well as the enemies within their own ranks, the communists. In 1929, a border conflict with the Soviet Union in the north of the country severely strained China's integrity and once again the Kuonmintang government lost control of the only recently pacified northern China. After a few more crises, the Soviet troops invaded Sianking, while, at the same time, British troops began to invade southern China. In 1937, there was a skirmish between the Chinese and Japanese soldiers, south-west of Beijing, leading to the second Japanese-Chinese war. Joseph Stalin appeared to be attempting to solve the internal conflicts, but he was actually trying to repair the relationship between the Kuonmintang and the CPC. The "Second United Front" resulted from pressure by the Soviet Union. It was purely tactical: The motivation of the Soviet dictator was immediately clear with the signing of the "Treaty of peace and friendship between Japan and the Soviet Union". Despite their previous conflicts, the nationalists of the Kuonmintang and the communists of the Soviet Union were provided with weapons and other materials. The treaty between the Soviet Union and Japan caused delivery of supplies to China to come to a halt and the country was left to fend for itself against Japan.

Behind the scenes of the "Second United Front" there was also trouble brewing: While the Kuonmintang bore the brunt of the war against Japan, the CPC reduced its participation to the minimum. Although the Japan-Chinese war officially finished as the Second World

War came to an end, on 9th September 1945, the "Second United Front" did not last much longer: In early 1946 the cooperation broke apart. It was not a great problem for the Kuonmintang: At the end of the Second World War, the Soviet Union was asked by the other allied forces to officially recognise the Kuonmintang government. They did as they were requested.

THE BIRTH OF THE PEOPLE'S REPUBLIC

In reality, the picture was completely different: Stalin supported the Chinese communists with a great deal of financial assistance. Through this support, which was carried out in extreme secrecy, the CPC began to fight a guerrilla war with the Kuonmintang. In 1949, the CPC had become so strong that it was finally able to prevail over the Kuonmintang. In the meantime, they had become known as the People's Liberation Army. The nationalists fled to Taiwan and founded there the Republic of China, which even today is only recognised by a small number of states. On the Chinese mainland, on the other hand, the state, which still exists today, was created with the People's Republic of China. The leader of the communist party and founder of the new state is one of the most important people in the history of China: Mao Zedong.

EXCURSUS: MAO ZEDONG – THE SUPERSTAR OF CHINA

Mao Zedong (1893-1976) was politician, leader of the party and, up to his death, the undisputed leader of the People's Republic of China. Mao came from a poor background and his father, a tradesman, always wanted his son to be a great man. That is why he gave him the name Zedong, which means something like "Benefactor of the east". He visited a Confucian school, which he left at the age of 13 because he was afraid of his teacher. After his change of school, he became assistant librarian at the University of Beijing. Here, he met people who taught him the fundamental concepts about Marxism and Leninism. He became increasingly interested in politics and wrote his first papers about the subject. Later, he worked as a junior school teacher in Changsha. As far back as 1921 he took part in the 1st party convention of the Communist Party of China but at that time, he played only a very small role. Mao established unions, organised strikes and led the workers. In 1923 he was asked to join the Central Committee; in 1925 he propagated a peasant uprising. That time in China was characterised by many conflicts. However, almost 20 years later, Mao became the Chairman of the Central Committee of the CPC and a personality cult grew up around him. In October, 1949, he proclaimed the People's Republic of China.

Between 1954 and 1958 Mao was the State President. After his resignation, he remained Chairman and the most powerful man in the country. In 1959, he managed the industrial programme called "The great leap forward" and in 1966 he called for the "Great Proletarian Cultural Revolution". After 1971, Mao did not show himself in public, it was assumed that he had become very sick. However, in January of 1975, he received Franz-Josef Strauß, the Chairman of the Christian Democratic Union of Germany. In October of the same year, he was visited by Helmut Schmidt. On 9th September, 1976, Mao died. His death caused deep distress within the population.

When the Communist Party of China founded the People's Republic of China with Mao at its head, there was a great deal of support from the population. As so often in the eventful history of the country, the economy was in ruins. However, the CPC were successful in their reforms, which included measures against inflation and a destroyed infrastructure. The people liked their obvious progress and it made the CPC very popular. For the first time in their eventful history, the Chinese communists were able to offer some form of stability and, above all, peace. Even today, China cannot be seen as a politically and socially united nation. There are many ethnic and cultural differences, as well as the "petit bourgeois", the "middle peasants" and the proletarians, to name but a few. Mao relied on the support of all these people to be successful. The communist leader permitted the establishment of eight parties to at least give the impression of having a democracy in the country. This in no way meant that they had any political influence. The true and absolute power was maintained by the CPC. Mao himself thought of this form of government as "democratic dictatorship". The principle was successful as the people felt that the problem of feeding the population had been solved by the 1950s. The economic situation was also thought to be solid: Social systems were established and industry and farming was recovering. Mao was able to establish a stable administrative structure. All these advances brought the party a great deal of popularity and the people slowly began to perceive themselves from a more a communist perspective. This was most noticeable in education. From childhood onwards, the people were subject to socialist doctrines. The aim was to create an intellectual elite, which was capable of developing the state ideologically.

The main goal of the communists was the removal of the feudal social structure which had prevailed since the times of the old republic and the Imperial Era. For this purpose, massive campaigns were carried out and the confiscation of land began. Under these reforms, the land was taken away from its previous owners and redistributed among those who had nothing. They used ruthless methods. Followers of the old systems of the Republic of China were sentenced to death.

In order to stabilise the flourishing economy, Mao and his party created the first "five-year-plan", which had its main emphasis on the development of heavy industry. With Soviet help, the annual economic growth was to be increased by up to nine percent. The financial burden of this industrial growth was to be borne by the agricultural income. At the same time, the re-structuring of this country was continuing. Small companies were bought off by the government. Even though these were promised support at the inception of the People's republic, the owners of these small businesses found themselves more or less forced into giving them up. The government bought up these companies and made the previous owners into the managers of them, under the direct control and supervision of the CPC. The companies thus became state-owned businesses.

From 1957, the government forced a further round of industrialisation. The farmers, who had been forced to participate in the industrialisation again had an important role to play. The result was the mass campaign called "Great Leap Forward".

The "Great Leap Forward" was a new economic road map, planned by the Mao government, which had the aim of equalising the rural and industrial economies to the same rate of success. Industrial production was strongly oriented on the economic success of western nations. At that time, the country was having a hard time. The financial and technical help that China was receiving from the Soviet Union made them economically dependent upon them.

The Chinese workers were not able to operate the highly modern industrial equipment of the time, which had been provided by their Soviet neighbours. The machinery was of a high technical standard which did not need many people to work it. That was not in line with the communist leadership's plans to focus on employment of the masses. Because of the uprisings in Poland and Hungary in 1956, the Soviet Union felt compelled to involve themselves more in European affairs. The result was that the assistance which they had been giving to China was being reduced. At the same time, there was unrest amongst the peasantry, which made up 75 percent of the population. The initial euphoria about the socialist turnaround had given way to disillusionment. The reason for the discontentment was exactly that success: By solving the feeding problem, the farmers were able to draw on better resources. Medical care was also available. These basic improvements in people's lives led to a higher birth-rate and a lower rate of childhood deaths. These positive developments were in conflict with the fact that the farmers did not feel any benefit from the land reforms. The large landowners were gone but the financial burdens had not reduced;

instead of paying the owners of the land, the tenants had to pay the state, large families paid the same amount for their food as they did before. In effect, there was not a great and palpable benefit with the new system. The communist regime lost favour with the population. At that point, the word "regime" had become appropriate. More and more officials of the CPC no longer saw themselves in the classical role of "servers of the people", but as the ruling class.

The establishment of people's communes was to be the solution to these various problems. Instead of gigantic production facilities, the communes were urged to produce their own urgently needed goods themselves. In that way, long transport journeys were avoided and direct access to goods of all kinds could be guaranteed. This new concept was meant to "bring the town into the country", and was designed to allow self-sufficiency to small farmers and to distance themselves from the party leaders in the bigger towns which had been so active up to then.

At first, the people's communes built up simple industrial plants. The farmers living close by gave up their land and the economic development was based on specialisation and work distribution. Forming the collectives brought significant problems with it. Those farmers who were assigned to industrial and infrastructure projects could not work much on their farms. The result was that the agricultural yield dropped, causing a shortage of food and catastrophic famine. In addition, part of their harvest had to be donated to the state. As well as the difficult internal politics existing at the time, there were also natural disasters, such as floods, which destroyed part of their harvests. Between the years 1959 and 1961 approximately 45 million people died from malnutrition.

In 1961 there was a new low in the history of China. The famine catastrophe caused industrial production to fail. The communist leaders responded with an emergency programme. This had positive results for about two-thirds of the industrial workers, who were permanently employed, with a workplace guarantee and health insurance. The other third of the industrial workers were the losers, who only received temporary work contracts. There was no social security for those workers, which caused an even greater discrepancy between the rich and the poor.

Irregularities among the leaders of the party, such as corruption, were dealt with by a new reform of Mao Zedong called the "Cultural Revolution". This meant that many of the communist officials lost their jobs. Only about one in four of those officials were able to keep their jobs after the reform. This was something which greatly met the approval of the people. One of the main points about the Cultural Revolution was that there were to be no agricultural or industrial changes made, in contrast to previous programmes. Mao understood that production had to run with as little interference as possible. Universities, schools and politics, however, were subject to huge transformations. Universities were closed at the beginning of the reforms, and not opened again until after the death of Mao Zedong and the end of the Cultural Revolution in 1978. Mao died in 1976 and did not live to see the end of the Cultural Revolution. Originally, the programme was only due to last for six months, but it did not end for the next ten years. Like many things in Chinese politics, there were a lot of contradictions. This could be seen in foreign policy, as an example. Disagreements with the Soviet Union led to a closer relationship with the USA, which in turn was contradictory to the Chinese ideology of a communist world.

After Mao's death, the Chinese went through another period of reform and liberalisation. This was mainly due to Mao Zedong's successor, a politician called Deng Xiaoping. Chinese leaders became more interested in experimenting around the political principle of a socialist market economy. Special economic zones were created on the coast and the people's communities were disbanded. This marked a turning point in Chinese history. Since then, China has become one of the fastest growing economies in the world. This in no way solved the problems within the country. The growing disparity between the rich and the poor and corruption, right up to the highest governmental levels, rekindled discussions about the future of China. Democratic movements were suppressed with force. An example for that was the massacre in the Square of Heavenly Peace (Tiananmen Square) in 1989. Deng Xiaoping died in 1997 and Jiang Zemin took his place.

As a further sign of opening-up, China was admitted into the World Trade Organisation (WTO). That was called the "third generation" and was followed in 2002 by the founder of the "fourth generation" led by Hu Jintao. Since then, the country has opened-up even more and is enjoying an economic boom. In 2010, China overtook their competitor, Japan, to become the worldwide greatest economic power, after the USA. Xi Jinping has been the General Secretary of the communist party and took over leadership of the People's Republic in the "fifth generation" in 2012. Despite its opening-up and its international trade, the People's Republic under Xi Jinping is far from being a democracy. In particular, critics of the political system are subject to state repression and human rights in the country are under threat.

- Chapter 2 -

THE CURRENT POLITICAL SYSTEM IN CHINA

A SUMMARY

The people of China regard their system as being a democracy, a form of government with represen-tatives elected by the people. At least, that is how we see democracy in a western world with liberal basic structures. The magazine "The Economist" publishes its democracy index once per year. A group of experts evaluate the conditions in various countries into the following categories: Electoral systems, pluralism, operating procedures of the government, political participation, political culture and civil rights. The Federal Republic of Germany is in 13th place in this world ranking and is considered to be a full democracy. The People's Republic of China landed at number 153 out of 167 countries in total. Based on the above statistic, there no longer seems to be a question of China having a living democracy: In China, there is an authoritarian-led regime. The leadership is with the communist party, and the state system is, at the same time, the internal party system. Formally, there are eight other parties which are in existence but not really considered as opposition as opposition is not required in this system. Those parties existing outside the CPC merely have an advisory role, at the very most.

It is clear who has the power of decision-making in China. Also, within the party, the most important institution is the politburo of the CPC, which is made up of 20 high-ranking officials, and the Central Committee of the CPC with a further 150 to 200 members. The most powerful man in the state is the chairman of the standing committee of the politburo of the CPC. The Chairmanship covers all the highest offices in the state, politics and military. Up to 2020, this post has been held by Xi Jinping. It is self-evident that this leader has to be be chosen from the ranks of the CPC. Elections as we know them do not exist. The successors are chosen from within the party. It is not possible for another party to offer an opposing candidate. Those other parties ae not even allowed by law to take any part in political events.

The eight parties are:

- Revolutionary Committee of the Chinese Kuomintang (RCCK)

- China Democratic League (CDL)

- China Democratic National Construction Association (CDNCA)

- China Zhi Gong Party (CZGP) (Public Interest Party of China)

- Taiwan Democratic Self-Government League (TDSGL)

- Chinese Peasants' and Workers' Democratic Party (CPWDP)

- China Association for Promoting Democracy (CAPD)

- Jiusan Society (JS) (Corporation of 3rd September)

As previously mentioned, these parties are of very little importance. Only once per year, at the General

Assembly of the Chinese People's Political Consultative Conference, these other Chinese political parties are able to show themselves to the public. The power difference between the communist party and the other parties is clearly demonstrated by the number of their members. While the CPC has almost 90 million members, the other parties can only show memberships in the low six-figure range.

FORMAL STRUCTURE OF THE GOVERNMENT

China's governmental system can be divided into two parts: These are the state and the party divisions. The state represents the formal and "official" division, but its existence is not conceivable without the party division. Using its power as a unity party, the CPC permeates all parts of the state apparatus.

The parliament of the People's Republic of China is the National People's Congress, which elects its State President, the State Council, the Supreme People's Court, the Central Military Commission and the National Supervisory Commission. The National People's Congress is enormous: Around 3000 representatives belong to this body and that is the reason why it only takes place once a year. The "substitute congress" is the Standing Committee of the National People's Congress, which regulates most affairs and is the real decision-making power of the state. Its 150 members supervise the work of the above-mentioned institutions, which have been elected by Congress (de facto by the Standing Committee).

The Chairman of the Standing Committee is the State President, who is also the State leader. At present, this is Xi Jinping. The State President has very broad powers. He makes laws, which are ratified by the People's Congress. He nominates and terminates the prime minister, who is the head of the State Council, the central committee of the people's republic. The State President also has the power to mobilise the military and ratify treaties with other States.

The State President can theoretically be any Chinese citizen who has completed his 45th year of life. His term of office is five years. A State President can be re-elected indefinitely. It was not always like that: The clause in the constitution, which prevented numerous re-elections, was repealed in 2018.

ADMINISTRATIVE STRUCTURE

China is a unitary state with its emphasis on centralisation. There are 23 provinces in total (including Taiwan), 4 cities, all directly under the control of the central government (Beijing, Tianjin, Chongqing and Shanghai), 333 regions, 2,860 districts and 41,040 townships. Inner Mongolia, Guanxi, Ningxia, Xinjiang and Tibet are all autonomous regions. There are 2 special administrative regions, Hongkong and Macau. Below the townships, there are village committees, who have the lowest administrative rank. This level of administration carries a lot of importance as here political decisions, made at the higher levels, are put into practice. At the village level the postal service is organised as well as the population census.

THE POPULATION OF CHINA

The People's Republic of China is the most populated country in the world. The number of people living in China in 2018 was said to be about 1.4 billion inhabitants, although this varies from institution to institution. The United Nations reported a population of 1.415 billion, whereas the CIA – the secret service of the United States – estimates the total population as 1.384 billion inhabitants. The State Agency for Statistics of the People's Republic of China has also published its figures: They estimate a population of 1.395 billion. No matter which figures you use, China remains the most populated country in the world. About 18 – 20% of the total world's inhabitants live in China – every fifth person in the world is therefore a Chinese citizen. However, this title is no longer unchallenged. The second most populated country is India, who is not far behind. According to the United Nations, that southern Asian country has about 1.3 billion inhabitants. Due to the rapid population development in India, it could overtake China to be the most populated county on earth by 2022.

China has always had a high population throughout its long history. There were no official censuses in China until 1953, but historians estimate that the country always had about 15% of the world's inhabitants. At the first census, in 1953, about 580 million people were registered – estimates were originally made at only 510 million but due to the sheer size of the population, there are bound to be a high number of unreported inhabitants, even today. Therefore, estimates have a discrepancy of up to 100 million people. There are also suggestions that the numbers recorded in the past must have been amended. Censuses are carried out regularly every 10 years in China. The next one is planned for 2020.

Decades ago, China carried out measures to control the population explosion, such as is now happening in India.

EXCURSUS: REWARDS FOR SMALL FAMILIES
The one-child policy is probably the single, most controversial measure that China has taken to control population growth. The name is self-explanatory: Each family is only allowed to have one child. However, there were a large number

of exceptions and special regulations too. The residential area of the family was also of importance. In urban areas, the one-child policy was controlled much more strongly than it was in the country. Contravening the rules was met with rigorous penalties. Those who kept to the rules enjoyed many benefits, such as rent allowances or free childcare places. In 2013, the one-child policy was relaxed, and it was abandoned altogether in 2016. Now a couple is allowed to have two children.

The plan to stabilise the population at 1.2 billion inhabitants by the year 2000 could not be realised. However, Chinese demographers estimate that the population will reach its peak of 1.44 billion people by the year 2029. After that, scientists believe that the population will reduce, as it has done with western industrial nations. The main reasons for this include the aging population and the effects of the one-child policy. There will also be an impact on China's economy, as it is estimated that more than 40% of the Chinese population will be over 60 by 2050. This means a massive loss of workforce, which has to be compensated for. The population is very unevenly spread. Significantly more people live in the urban centres of the east and south east of the country. The most highly populated centres are Guangzhou, Hongkong, Shenzhen, Dongguan, Shanghai, Nanjing and Suzhou. In contrast, there are wide areas of the west and north of China which are practically uninhabited. This development is not new: 9% of the total Chinese population was already living in the eastern part of China by 1982. In the People's Republic there are 15 megacities with populations of over 10 million people, most of all the metropolitan region of Shanghai. In addition, there are a further 150 large cities with populations of over 1 million people.

The ten biggest cities in 2010 were:

1. Shanghai   20.2 MM inhabitants
2. Beijing   16.4 MM inhabitants
3. Guangzhou   10.6 MM inhabitants
4. Shenzhen   10.3 MM inhabitants
5. Tianjin   9.2 MM inhabitants
6. Wuhan   7.5 MM inhabitants
7. Dongguan   7.2 MM inhabitants
8. Foshan   6.7 MM inhabitants
9. Chengdu   6.3 MM inhabitants

10. Chongqing   6.2 MM inhabitants

(Note: Hongkong would be in 8th place with its 6.7 MM inhabitants. However, due to its status as a special administrative zone, it is not included in the list.)

China is a country of immigration as well as emigration, although the number of emigrants outnumbers the immigrants ten to one. As a proportion of the total population of the country, the number of Chinese living abroad, as well as the number of foreigners living in China is relatively small: In 2016 one immigrant could be counted for every 1000 Chinese nationals, making a quota of 0.1 percent. Most of the people who immigrated to China came from Korea, the Philippines or Brazil. The typical countries for Chinese to emigrate to include the United States of America, South Korea and Japan. About 9.6 million Chinese live abroad and are more or less assimilated into their chosen country. It is important to note that the state views people living in the Chinese special administration zones, such as Hongkong, as foreign.

EXCURSUS: NOT LIKE IN THE FILMS: THE CHINATOWNS.

Chinatowns are famous and notorious at the same time. Chinatowns are neighbourhoods, at the fringes of large cities, which are largely populated by Chinese, who at one time or another turned their backs on "their" People's Republic and emigrated. Often the families living there are in the second or third generations and most of the commercial landscape leans towards gastronomy. A large number of neon adver-tisements and signs in Chinese symbols indicate premises selling Chinese specialities. That is how it looks in the gangster films of Hollywood. In reality, Chinatowns often look very different. They are not only to be found in the USA but everywhere in the world, such as in South America or Africa. People living in those regions are mainly of Chinese origin but their cultural significance has been in decline over recent years. Chinatowns are no longer really neighbourhoods, but more like single streets with rows of Chinese shops. That is what it looks like in New York, for example. By the way, there are also Chinatowns in Germany, such as in Berlin.

RELIGION IN CHINA

China is a multi-ethnic and multi-religious country. Many different religions exist in the People's Republic, side by side. The five most important religions are Buddhism, Taoism, Islam, as well as Catholic and protestant Christianity. Taoism is the only one of the above-mentioned religions which originates in China. The others are "imported" and arrived in China due to population movement from all different parts of the world. Buddhism can be traced back to about 100 BC, Islam arrived in 700 - 800 AD, during the Imperial Era of China. The Chinese people came into contact with Christianity around 1200 AD. All five religions are accepted under the communist directive. However, Catholicism and Protestantism are not combined under the generic term "Christianity". Both are considered to be independent religions. The right to religious freedom is anchored into the country's constitution, faith and state are strictly separated. In this way, every citizen is free to practise the religion of his choice. That is how it is written in the constitution. However, in reality, these rights are often restricted. In addition, it is expected of the inhabitants that they do not publicly or officially profess to a religion. This means that they are not officially registered with a particular religion. Although there are about 85,000 religious centres of all denominations across the land, there are no reliable numbers of each faith recorded. It is unusual for Chinese to profess to a particular religion and the characteristics of the various religions are often mixed up. People say about the Chinese, as they indeed say about themselves, that they practise a certain religious pragmatism. They choose their brand of religion based on their personal situation. This behaviour is the subject of several Chinese proverbs. Because of that, there is no uniform religion in China. This allows the Chinese to have a number of ideological and philosophical perspectives at the same time.

UNDERSTANDING OF DEMOCRACY

The majority of the Chinese population think of themselves as being part of a democratic state. The reason for this is that their understanding of democracy is very different from that of western countries. Instead of having a liberal democratic constitution, liberal economic processes, a sharing of power between the judiciary, legislative and executive branches, and the ability to have free elections, China sees their country as predominantly a protectorate. In accordance with the ideological tradition, a state is there to protect its people. For that reason, a government must consist of particularly virtuous, morally acting and educated people. These characteristics are thought to be obligatory prerequisites by the majority of the population. Because of this, the people have "voluntarily" waived their rights to democracy and political co-determination, such as referenda. The people have great faith in the politicians of the highest level. Their skills are believed to enable them to govern on behalf of the common good and they enjoy great powers in order to enforce that common good. The amount of trust afforded to them means that the Chinese see no justification for resistance against the state. This is comparable with the ideal image of a "wise king", who is only there to serve his people. In reverse, the Chinese expect that the government listens to - and respects – the opinion of the people and acts accordingly.

EXCURSUS: UIGHURS IN CHINA

The Uighurs originally come from central Asia. Today about 45 percent of the 23,600,000 inhabitants of Xinjiang, an autonomic region of China, are members of the Turk people, making them the biggest ethnic group in that city. In 1949, after the victory of the communists in the Chinese civil war, the region was taken over by the People's Republic. However, many special rights aimed at self-fulfilment were granted to the Uighurs, allowing them certain freedoms, but there were also disadvantages. Democratic movements within the Uighur minority were immediately quashed and many rebellions followed. There was great unrest in 1990, 1997, 2009 and 2014 resulting in many fatalities.

The Uighurs are trying to make an independent state for themselves, which would be called East Turkestan. Their attempts at achieving complete separation from the People's Republic are not always peaceful: The "East Turkestan Islamic Movement", ETIM for short, has been classified as a terrorist organisation and is said to be allied to Al-Qaeda and the Taliban. The behaviour of the Chinese authorities is also not free of criticism. Many observers report a systematic repression of the Uighurs. Random arrests are common, religious sites of the Uighur Muslims have been destroyed.

There is also talk of "re-education camps", where Uighurs are being re-educated to "real Chinese", in violation of human rights. These actions are often legitimised as a "fight against terror".

THE CHINESE JUDICIAL SYSTEM

The judicial system of the People's Republic differs from that of the German system in many respects. The separation of power between the legislative, judiciary and executive functions is unknown. Legal differences are dealt with by the so-called People's Courts, which are the institutions responsible for jurisdiction. There are such courts at every level, the highest authority being the People's Court based in Beijing. All other People's Courts are subordinate to that one, which supervises and ensures that the rule of law is followed. Candidates for judge positions are subject to stiff checks and public scrutiny. During this selection procedure, it is not only their professional qualities which are scrutinised but also their political behaviour and party conformity.

In the recent past, the Chinese government has been moving towards an international rule of law, orienting itself more towards international standards. This has enabled a certain amount of legal protection to be established. Even if the Chinese laws are based on western models, the population is still subject to the guidelines of the communist party. This means that judicial independence is not ensured.

The Chinese government is often accused of human rights violations. Particularly after the massacre on the Square of Heavenly Peace in 1989, the subject of human rights has come into sharper focus and it has made the Chinese relationship with its international partners very difficult. Relationships with the European Union are particularly strained as a result of human rights violations. Organisations, such as Amnesty International accuse the Chinese government of abusing even the most fundamental of human rights.

According to the Chinese Constitution, human rights are supposed to be guaranteed and as such are defined in Article 22, Paragraph 3 of the document. In reality, the idea of human rights is interpreted differently in China than in other states. From a Chinese point of view, the increase in prosperity of the general population is more important than the protection of an individual. Constitutionally, the Chinese believe that human rights are afforded by the state and are protected. The rights of individuals may not violate the rights of others or the interest of the state or community. Apart from that, human rights are not "cost-free", they must be set against the duty to the state or community. China is one of the few countries in the world which still carries out the death penalty. This form of punishment is also carried out on delinquent minors, which has been heavily criticised by Amnesty International. The human rights organisation also accuses China of performing the highest number of executions, worldwide. However, this is refuted by the government in Beijing. The local People's Courts also have a great amount of autonomy regarding punishment, and are also permitted to issue the death penalty, which can be applied for a large number of possible crimes. Murder is not the only offence which is punishable by death, the list also includes rape, kidnapping and drug offences. There are also reports of the death sentence being pronounced for adultery, although this is said to be exceptional in China. Since 2007, the number of offences which carry the death penalty has been reduced to only a few. Up to that point, the local People's Courts could decide for themselves what offences were punishable by death. Since 2007, all executions must be confirmed by the Supreme Court. In 2011 the arbitrary imposition of capital punishment was restricted and the Supreme Court reduced the number of offences, which could be punishable by death, to 50. These include violent crime, manslaughter, human trafficking, sabotage and espionage. The theft of organs and the preparation and distribution of fake medicines also fall under the definition of capital offences. The death penalty is explicitly forbidden for political crimes, although this was not always the case. Nowadays, those who are younger than 18 at the time of the incident, pregnant women and people over the age of 75 are excepted from the death penalty. In 2011, the Chinese government stated that the total abolition of the death penalty was an important aim. The international community has reported that the number of executions has been reduced, step by step. The ultimate aim is also to abolish forced labour and torture altogether.

EXCURSUS: GERMAN LAWS FOR CHINESE CITIZENS

The People's Republic wants to be known as a constitutional state and has, over the last few years, invited many experts from abroad to help them to achieve it. This help is mainly coming from Germany – from the GIZ – The German Society for International Cooperation. While working on the definitions for the new constitutional state, they have relied heavily on the "Bürgerlichen Gesetzbuch" (BGB) – The German civil code. Practically, the whole of the BGB has been adopted. However, the implementation of the laws does not work as well as it does in Germany. Despite that, the project is considered to be an important collaboration, which is not comparable to any other cooperation on earth.

CHINA'S FOREIGN POLICY

China represents its own interest with a great deal of self-confidence. Basically, China wants to be part of the solution on global issues. The People's Republic is a nuclear power, one of the largest economic states and is a full-time member of the United Nations. China is a member of the G20 states, the twenty most important industrial and emerging countries, together with the United States of America, the European Union, Germany, France, the United Kingdom, India, Argentina, Australia, Brazil, Indonesia, Turkey, Canada, Mexico, South Korea, Russia, Saudi Arabia, Italy, South Africa and Japan.

China is focusing on its own development processes, stabilising the region, secure trade routes and a deepening of the relationship towards USA, Russia, the European Union and its neighbouring states.

EXCURSUS: CHINA AND GERMANY: CONTINUAL DIALOGUE

The People's Republic of China and Germany have not crossed paths in history many times. It was not until 1972 that diplomatic relations were established. Since then, however, the relationship between the two states has steadily increased and now China is one of Germany's most important trade partners. Together, using the programme called "Comprehensive Strategic Partnership", they have overcome several crises. China considers Germany to be THE partner in the EU: There is intensive cooperation in the areas of environmental policy, trade, science and culture. The relationship is stable and good.

Despite the spirit of fellowship, there are some discrepancies. For example, one point of constant criticism of Germany towards China is the question of human rights. Germany demands reinforcement of those rights and seeks dialogue repeatedly.

The relationship between the People's Republic of China and the United States of America is particularly important. China's government signalled that it is very interested in having a strong working relationship between the two states. A bad trade relationship would have devastating consequences, considering how closely the two countries are entwined financially.

There are significant differences already. A big regional problem is the potential nuclear threat coming from North Korea, with whom China traditionally has a close relationship. In 2017, after the rocket tests in North Korea, the USA installed a rocket missile defence system in South Korea. This caused a breakdown in the relationship between China and the USA. South Korea has been hit hardest by these developments. After a rivalry which existed between China and South Korea, which lasted many years, since 2013 the countries have tried to repair their relationship. However, the missile defence system, built by the USA, caused the Chinese government to feel threatened and since then the relationship between China and South Korea has once again become unstable. South Korea is one of the USA's closest allies. Despite these events, the relationship between China and their North Korean neighbours is not particularly close. Because of the rocket testing, which represent a threat to China, the People's Republic agreed to increased sanctions against North Korea, together with the United Nations. North Korean companies were closed and the import of coal was severely limited. With that, North Korea lost one of its most important sources of income. The Chinese, however, wanted to avoid imposing a full

economic boycott, so as not to risk the collapse of the
Chinese economy. As a solution out of that difficult
situation, the Chinese are maintaining strong ties with
both the USA and North Korea.

North Korean ? *(handwritten margin note)*

For centuries, the relationship between China and
Russia has been difficult. At present, it could be
described as co-operative. Both sides are aiming to
provide an economic counter-balance to the USA.
Russia is China's most important partner in the arms
industry and is interested in receiving deliveries of
Russian gas, oil and electricity.

The relationship between Japan and China has been
marred for centuries by countless military conflicts and
they have developed a rivalry which has continued to
grow over the years. Today, their relationship could be
considered ambivalent, which manifests itself in the
mistrust which they each harbour for the other. There
are often conflicts caused by the presence of ships,
from both China and Japan, in waters which they each
claim to be their own.

EXCURSUS: TERRITORIAL CONFLICTS IN THE SOUTH CHINA SEA

The South China Sea is the home of many resources, extensive fishing grounds and a sheer incalculable number of islands where their political status is not clearly defined. The main reason for this is that the territorial claims of those islands were not contractually established after the Second World War. An example of the confusing political situation applies to the islands of Spratly, which are a group of islands spreading over an area of 1,000 miles, relatively close to the Philippines. The Spratly Islands were initially considered to be British territory. Later, they were claimed by the French, but even later, during the Second World War, were occupied by the Japanese. At the end of the war, the Chinese claimed them for themselves. The Chinese soldiers initially retreated but the islands remained under the control of the People's Republic. In 1968, the Philippian government claimed a part of the Spratly Islands which was close to the mainland as their own. The People's Republic then sent back the troops in 1980, resulting in the occupation of the Islands by the

Philippian armed forces. The situation became serious in 1988: The Chinese navy sank two Vietnamese ships when they began to show interest in claiming the Spratly Islands. In 1990, a further interested party appeared in the shape of Malaysia, who staked a claim for three of the Spratly Islands and promptly occupied them. Other interested parties in the group of islands included Brunei and Taiwan.

The reason for all the unrest was, that gigantic oil and ore deposits were suspected in the area. This group of islands was not the only area with ill-defined ownership. Further examples included the Senkaku Islands (claimed by China, Japan and Taiwan), the Paracel Islands (claimed by China and Vietnam), the Zhongsha Islands (claimed by China, the Philippines and Taiwan) and the Huangyan Dao Atoll (claimed by China and the Philippines).

While the relationship between India and China is more of a pragmatic nature, there is a close friendship between China and Pakistan. China is active in Pakistan and supports the government in the development of infrastructure projects. China is also working with Afghanistan in much the same way.

EXCURSUS: CHINAS INVOLVEMENT IN AFRICA

In recent years there have often been discussions regarding China's commitment towards Africa. Foreign trade and investments in energy and commodities are central to the economic relationship between China and Africa. In addition to projects aimed at securing resources, many other projects have been implemented, such as those in infrastructure, education, transfer of technology and foreign trade. To date, it is not clear what impact this will have on the economic development of the African countries. Nevertheless, there is a good deal of criticism levelled at China that they are forcing the African states into economic dependency by instructing Chinese companies to implement infrastructure projects financed by Chinese creditors. If these eager African states are unable to pay for their credit in the future, they will be helplessly dependent upon China's demands. However, it is still too early to judge the impact of China's presence in Africa.

HEALTH SYSTEM IN CHINA

During the 1970s, the Chinese health system was considered exemplary. To this day, hospitals are open to the public and are non-profit organisations. However, in reality, access to health care is denied to a great number of the people. Only about 5% of those living in rural areas of China have proper access to the benefits of the health system.

Resident physicians, as we know them in Germany, are seldom. About 90% of all treatments are carried out in the public hospitals, of which there are almost 30,000 throughout the country. In addition, there are a further 37,000 infirmaries and about 215,000 outpatient clinics. In total the People's Republic provides about seven million hospital beds. A particularly important part of everyday treatment is the traditional Chinese medicine. There are about 4,000 clinics which only treat patients in this way. TCM

EXCURSUS: PRACTITIONERS WITHOUT DEGREES:
THE BAREFOOT DOCTORS
Much of China's population lived (and still lives) in rural areas, where skilled workers are scarce;

this also applies to medical practitioners. When the treatment of a sickness or injury was urgent, they needed a solution. That was the birth of the barefoot doctor. They were, more or less, hobby doctors from agricultural collectives who used their knowledge of Traditional Chinese Medicine on their patients. These were in no way professional medical personnel and were more like healers, who travelled from village to village. They gave acupuncture and other household remedies instead of tablets. Not much is known about the amount of success they had and the results of their treatment were probably quite sobering. Nevertheless, the barefoot doctors were able to treat small injuries, give vaccinations and improve the hygiene in working areas. Also, the belief in the efficacy of Chinese Traditional Medicine will have done its part.

Hospitals can be divided into three classifications. The lower class offers more basic amenities, whereas the hospitals in the third or upper class have excellent amenities and are comparable with those of international standard. Unfortunately, it is clear that only the smallest minority of the population can enjoy this level of care. A large number of people still have no access to any medical care. In order to make that standard of care available to a larger section of the population, there are several reforms in progress. By the end of 2020, it is hoped that every citizen will have access to at least basic health care. The outbreak of the corona virus in 2019 and 2020 made plain that the health system was badly in need of reform. Even though the country's economy was quickly able to build up a medical infrastructure to deal with the infection, this emergency laid bare how badly the Chinese medical system was able to deal with the outbreak.

EXCURSUS: A HOSPITAL IN A WEEK

At the end of December, 2019, the corona virus broke out in the province of Wuhan. The Chinese government demonstrated its will to fight the virus using an immense volume of people and material. Where there is a will, there is a way: Excavators fast-tracked the building of a hospital out of thin air in just one week. The Hounshenshan Hospital had 1,000 beds and required the employment of 7,500 building workers. A second hospital, similar to the first, followed. That one was even bigger, with 1,600 beds. About 1,400 medical personnel found work there in just one week.

Even though there are a lot of weaknesses in the Chinese health system, China cannot be considered a developing country in this respect. A publication from the Communist Party from 2016 states that the average life expectancy in China is 76 years. The report also states that they are expecting an increase in life expectancy to 79 years in the future. For the first time, the so-called "diseases of affluence" are reported, which have become part of Chinese society since there has been an increase in standard of living and income. Between 1978 and 2015 China had doubled its investment in the health system; costs have risen from three to six percent of the gross domestic product.

- Chapter 3 -

THE EDUCATION SYSTEM IN CHINA

BACKGROUND TO THE EDUCATIONAL SYSTEM.

As already mentioned, the structures in China are highly decentralised. This is also true of the educational system. Each province has a decisive voice in the interpretation of the laws regarding the schooling system. The Ministry for Education is the highest authority in the People's Republic. However, in view of the significant decision-making rights of the provinces and autonomous regions, the influence of the supreme authority is not particularly great. As with many administrative functions of the People's Republic, the responsibilities are shifted from the upper to the lower levels of administration. Just as the areas of finance, personnel and content planning are more or less autonomous in the provinces, so too is the education sector.

The educational system in China has been standardised, in line with that of the ISCED (International Standard Classification) of the UNESCO. This classification of school types and systems of the international school system is separated into various levels, therefore rendering them comparable with the education standards of the other countries. The international standardisation of the schools, together with the participation of the worldwide educational programme "Education For All" (EFS), which is also managed by UNESCO, has enabled the Chinese government to report a literacy rate of 98%. In 2006 the educational system and the law of compulsory education was reformed. Changes included a complete waiver of school fees including fees for extra tuition. All provincial authorities have to abide by that basic principle. The Chinese educational system can be regarded as successful. By international standards, for example in the PISA study, the Chinese schools attained very good scores.

KINDERGARTEN

At the beginning of their academic education, children may be sent to the (kindergarten) Participation is voluntary and the parents can decide at which age their children can go. The minimum age for entry is three years. Chinese children must leave the kindergarten at the age of seven and they must then attend primary school.

Chinese kindergartens follow similar concepts to those in Germany. There is a choice between half-day or full-day care, and it is also possible to bring a child for just a few hours. The purpose of the kindergarten is to prepare the children for primary school, taking into consideration their age and emotional upbringing. Inside the kindergarten, the children are divided into larger groups: Groups of 35 children are not unusual in China. Each group is supervised and managed by several pre-school teachers; normally about three educators per group. Kindergartens are paid for much as they are in western countries. The state does not pay for these establishments, it is likely that they are paid by the city, community, churches or privately. There are a lot of companies which offer crèche facilities for their employees. Costs for this service vary enormously. Although generally, a place in an urban kindergarten is more expensive than in the rural districts, there are other factors which play an important role. The age of the child, the time spent in the facility, what the facility offers and the parents' financial situation are decisive factors in the fees payable. In rural areas, the situation is slightly different: Often, the fees are paid by the provinces, eliminating the cost to the parents completely. The same applies for rural company-run kindergarten systems, which are normally free of charge.

PRIMARY SCHOOL

After their (voluntary) time at the kindergarten, the children will attend the primary school, which is compulsory. This occurs at the age of six or seven years, similar to Germany. The length of primary school attendance is slightly longer than that of Germany: German children usually visit the primary school for four years, whereas in China, they attend for six years. Chinese children have a longer school week amounting to 26 – 30 lessons of 50 minutes each. They are taught Chinese, mathematics, art, sport, science and music. After the third school year, English is taught.

In everyday schooling in China, the individuality of the student is taken into consideration and actively encouraged. The aim is to bring about independence and autonomic thought processes. Optically, this autonomy is not really desired: In most Chinese primary schools, wearing school uniform is compulsory.

MIDDLE SCHOOL

The next level in Chinese schooling is secondary education at the middle school. Secondary education is divided into two parts, junior middle and senior middle, each lasting three years. This corresponds to classes seven to nine at the junior level and ten to twelve at the senior level. In China, therefore, the junior middle is comparable with the German middle school, making the total length of education in the Chinese middle school six years. During this time, a certain amount of specialisation takes place. There are vocational, general and technical middle schools. The number of subjects taken increases during the middle school. There are also subjects which seem unusual to us, such as IT, technology and economic science. Natural sciences are taught in their separate disciplines. Chemistry, physics and biology are single subjects in the middle school in China. Ethnics is also a subject added to a weekly timetable which stretches 35 lessons at 45 minutes each. After three years at junior middle, students must take a final examination, which also serves as an entrance examination for the senior middle. On reaching senior middle, greater discipline is expected by the students. In addition to the 35 hours of schooling, there is a further compulsory two hours of self-study. In the eleventh class, students have the possibility to choose their future path between a humanities or a science programme.

At the end of the middle school, students must take the Gao Kao, the Chinese equivalent of the high school graduation examination (The Abitur in Germany or the Matura in Austria). It is the examination which is taken after 12 years of schooling and enables the student, if successful, to apply for a university place. The Gao Kao is a written examination; students can choose some of the subjects which are to be examined, but compulsory examinations are Chinese philology, mathematics and one foreign language (usually English). In addition, students can choose three more subjects either from the humanities or natural science sectors. The Gao Kao has a high significance, not only among the students but in society in general. At the time of the Gao Kao, which takes place annually on 7th June, the citizens and administration take care to provide a great deal of quiet, so that the examinees are able to get restful sleep during that period. It is not unusual for building work to be stopped during exam time, so as not to disturb the students. In addition, it is customary for the police to escort students to the Gao Kao if they are likely to be stuck in traffic jams. After all, it is in the interests of the Chinese society that the students arrive punctually for their end exams.

It is the job of the general middle schools to prepare the students for entrance to universities. In addition, there is a large number of middle schools which are specialised in preparing students for vocational training, and schooling takes place accordingly. For example, there is also a number of Buddhist or forestry schools. After compulsory studies lasting nine years – in normal schools it is 12 years – the student takes part in vocational training which usually lasts two to four years. Often the specialist schools are sponsored by large companies and so serve as talent pools. Their training plan is not defined by the authorities, but by the financing company. There they would learn to be skilled workers in, for example, the heavy, steel or oil industries.

UNIVERSITY

According to the Chinese Ministry of Education there are about 42 million students in the People's Republic per academic year. One of the most popular courses is engineering science. Almost one in every three students takes this course. Other popular subjects include management science, natural sciences generally, as well as art and medicine. Degrees obtained are not always recognised internationally, but a comprehensive reform brought improvements to the academic conditions. The Ministry of Education developed a project in 1995, called Project 211, which was intended to bring approximately one hundred Chinese high schools up to western levels of education by the turn of the millennium. The project was a resounding success. Now there are ten universities which can present themselves as top universities and which are comparable with international standards.

These include:

- Beijing University
- Tsinghua University
- Chinese People's University

- Sun Yat-Sen University
- Jiao Tong University in Xi'an
- The University of Nanjing
- Chinese University of Science and Techno-logy
- Fudan University
- Zhejiang University

There are many universities in all. According to the publication from the Ministry of Education, the total amounts to about 2,500 universities. It is interesting to note that only 75 of them are directly managed by the Ministry.

The entry conditions for a Chinese universities are extremely hard. Only the best students in the province will be allowed to take one of the sought-after places in these elite universities. There are also ideological hurdles to surmount. Even though the attendance at a university is not tied to being a member of the communist party, students must take part in a compulsory ideological course in the subjects of Marxism, Maoism, (Economic) politics and ethnicity before they are admitted into their university. This requirement is independent of which subject is being studied, even, as an example, physics students. The allocation of study places is carried out on a points system with respect to the numerus clauses, very much the same as in Germany. Even though there are no school fees in China's school system, study fees usually apply for university students. The fees are not regulated uniformly. Depending on the region and the reputation of the university, these can reach a maximum of the equivalent of 800 US Dollar per year per student. These fees, together with state funding, are the main sources of income for universities. Due to the wide range of cooperation between the universities and businesses, students are offered the opportunity to do their work experience within the companies. This provides various advantages for the universities, such as additional sources of income.

- Chapter 4 -

CHINA'S ECONOMY

GENERAL SUMMARY

China has become a true superpower as far as the economy is concerned. After the opening and reform politics, which started in 1978, the economy has been flourishing. In 2010, the People's Republic rose to become an international superpower, overtaking Japan, their greatest economic rivals in Asia. The gross domestic product (GDP) amounted to 11.2 billion US Dollars (2016). The GDP per capita totalled approximately 8,100 US Dollars. That puts China firmly in the middle range in international comparison.

China is the leading export country. Since the opening of the Chinese economy in the late 1970s, the export volume of 2 billion US Dollars at the time rose to 2,000 billion. There is no other country in the world presently able to produce so much agricultural product. China is also in first place in the list of great industrial countries. In total, some 900 million people have jobs in China.

China's thriving economy has also placed them in first place in the production sector and in the agricultural sector, the People's Republic has left many of its competitors behind in the global market. In 2016, China was the worldwide largest producer of grain, wheat, rice, apples, grapes, potatoes, fish, cotton, pork and mutton. As the country is rich in natural resources, their mining industry is also in top position. The worldwide largest amounts of gold, zinc, tin, lead and iron ore are mined in the People's Republic. In the industrial sector, China also leads in the production of iron, steel, aluminium, cement, cardboard, paper and fertiliser, and China is also the largest energy and electricity producer in the world.

These factors add up to a balance that is plain for all to see. It was not always like that, though. The boom in China was quick and successful. At the beginning of the People's Republic, the average wage was 54 US Dollars per person per year – not per month. At that time the People's Republic was one of the poorest countries on earth. However, the various reforms resulted in success in a relatively short time. Industrialisation in China provided a true surge in earnings. Living standards and prosperity improved abruptly at the beginning of the 1980s. According to the World Bank, the People's Republic is changing from a developing country into a land with an above average global income level. Life expectancy has increased and the level of education has risen visibly. In 2016, 43.4 million people were living in poverty. Bearing in mind that the total population is about 1.4 billion people, this is a comparatively low ratio.

State Leader Xi Jinping is trying to reduce this number further. Measures taken by the government included the creation of more jobs and the improvement of living standards, in particular in low-income areas. The intention is also to increase education and health in these regions in special projects. However, they did not achieve their goal of having a modest degree of prosperity for everyone by the year 2020. The real meaning of modest prosperity was not specifically defined.

The gap between rich and poor is very large. The most millionaires live together in Hongkong, in the most densely populated area in the world. This is not due to the Chinese government or the country's economy: As Hongkong was handed back to China by the United

Kingdom on 1st July 1997, the situation was very similar then. Macao is also known for its dense population of millionaires. It is said that a total of almost 720,000 millionaires are living in the People's Republic. A little more than 300 people are even richer and can call themselves billionaires.

In contrast to that, an average Chinese family earns between 80 to 800 US Dollars per month, depending on region and residential area. Those who have an annual income of between 10,000 and 30,000 US Dollars can be considered middle class. There are about 720 million people in China who fall within this bracket. This means that one in every two Chinese citizens belongs to the middle class. As previously mentioned, the wealth in China is very unevenly spread. The Chinese people have vented their anger at that point in a great number of protests.

The people of China are eligible for social security. This covers sickness, ageing costs, accidents, maternity needs and unemployment. Their social security ensures that they receive assistance to safeguard their existence. However, in reality, the state social security is not applied consistently. Only those who are employed are insured. Other people, such as students, children and self-employed are not eligible for this assistance. Also, those who live in rural regions do not receive assistance. The people in these groups can apply for voluntary insurance, of which half is paid by the state and they must pay the other half themselves.

In order to deal with poverty in the cities of the People's Republic, a state social assistance programme was introduced. This supports old or disabled people as well as children who have to grow up without their parents. This assistance usually comes in the form of services and items of value but in some cases cash payments are possible. The condition for receiving such assistance is that the disadvantaged persons have no possibility of receiving aid from their families. The Chinese know that before they can ask for support from the state, they must first ask for help from their relatives.

REGIONAL ECONOMIES

The economy is unequally distributed within the various regions and provinces of China. Generally, economic development has grown much quicker in the coastal regions, due to the higher availability of resources and workforce than can be found in the provinces. In these regions there is a higher prosperity among the people, with the earnings per head often many times greater than those in rural areas. The richest regions in China are said to be the Yangtze Delta, the Jingjinji region and the so-called Pearl River Delta. It is expected that the regions which are already responsible for the largest part of the economic success of China will continue to grow rapidly. This includes not only the economy but also the population. The Chinese government is trying to decrease, or at least simplify, the amount of bureaucracy, in order to maintain its growth.

Particularly between the 1970s and 2000s, China's economy has maintained a steady growth, and has been able to close the economic gap between them and their neighbouring states, such as Japan and South Korea. Both Japan and South Korea went through a similar development phase earlier in their history. Both are highly developed industrial nations today.

Since the 1980s, the surplus in China's trade balance has increased tenfold. Their industrial success was of a different nature at the beginning, particularly in the low-wage sector, where China established itself as a global payer, mainly in the textile industry. An example of this was the massive production of shoes. They have not left this sector completely, but today, China has long become established in the global marketing of automobiles, hardware and pharmaceuticals.

The positive development of the economy is seen by the government not only as desirable, but as an existential necessity. At the 11th Five Year Plan, the leadership promised a guaranteed annual economic growth of 8 percent. According to the government, such a growth is the only possibility of guaranteeing and improving the wealth of its people, further developing industry and closing the blatant inequality gap between rural and urban populations. Maintaining an economic growth of this nature is not only seen by experts as ambitious, courageous and at the same time extremely risky: It would be the first time in economic history that such targets would be successful. This poses the pressing question whether an economic growth of 8 percent is even possible to maintain. Economists believe they already know the answer. It would seem difficult, if not impossible, to maintain that course.

In the past there had been phases in the history of the People's Republic which allowed increased economic growth. One example of that was the change in direction from being an agricultural state into one of heavy industry. This was enforced by comprehensive reforms which were designed to reduce the effects of the centrally planned economy and even eliminate parts of it. This was the first and fundamental step towards opening the country to the global market. In the 1990s, the industrial sector was massively restructured. The changes always took place with the leadership of politicians, whose job it was to craft a unified economic path. In order for them to achieve a consistent economy, they repeatedly had to make more reforms. In that way, the financial economy became more liberal and the opening of the country for foreign investment and the development towards becoming a true capital market was facilitated. The opening of the country was considered to be a milestone in the development of ideological communism. It was, however, a necessary step towards the economic growth of the nation. Generally, the opening of the market was regarded as the only way left to generate the promised growth. In 2014, the government announced a reduced economic growth of 7.4 percent. It reacted with a series of new projects in order to stimulate the economy. Many new infrastructure projects were planned, including a new airport and railway network.

THE RENMINBI

The national currency of China is called the Renminbi. Translated, this means "people's money". However, you cannot go into a shop and buy a product for "XY Renminbi". This is only the name of the currency; the primary unit of currency is called the Yuan. This can be confusing because outside China most people speak about the "Chinese Yuan". The international currency code (ISO) does not help to clarify the situation either. The more usual abbreviation CNY suggests that the word "Yuan" refers to the actual currency. Another peculiarity is that the international symbol of the renminbi is the same as the Japanese Yen – a capital "Y" with two lines crossing it.

1 Yuan is divided into 10 Jiao, which in turn is divided into 10 Fen. The Renminbi is issued by the People's Bank of China. Many states have invested some money reserves in Renminbi. Apart from the People's Republic of China, the Renminbi is also used in other states, such as Laos, Cambodia, North Korea, Myanmar and Nepal, although they are not the official currencies in those countries. Up to 2005, the Renminbi was tied to the US Dollar. However, this was relinquished at the opening-

up of the free market economy in order to make Chinese industry more competitive.

The International Monetary Fund has listed the Renminbi as a major global currency since 2015, together with the US Dollar, the Euro, the British Pound and the Japanese Yen.

CHINA'S AGRICULTURE

China has become the world's undisputed number one in agriculture. The People's Republic is also its own largest consumer of agricultural products. About 300 million people work on the land. Unused farmland is almost impossible to find. Practically every spot of earth is used to farm foods. In a global comparison, China is the largest producer of wheat, corn, tobacco, barley, soy beans, millet, potatoes, peanuts among others. Farming is carried out efficiently and intensively. Despite its lack of landmass, China has overtaken the long-time market segment leader, USA in agricultural production, using its own special methods. One reason for the long-term success has been the increase in mechanisation and work processes which is greatly encouraged by the government. The Chinese officials hope to increase their yields in the future using special fertilisers and techniques. China's efficiency has also been noticed by other institutions, such as the World Food Programme of the United Nations. With a quota of only seven percent of the world's farmlands, China produces about 20 percent of the total food requirements.

Livestock farming is an important branch of the Chinese agricultural economy. The People's Republic is the world's leading producer of chicken (and eggs) and pork. Even though other countries produce more beef and lamb than China, the capacity of the People's Republic here is enormous. There is much importance attached to the fish industry. Great investments have been made in fish farming and aquaculture so that China has become the worldwide largest producer of fish products. A larger – although decreasing – part of that comes from sea fishing. Over-fishing has reduced the fish stocks greatly and some breeds of fish are endangered.

FOREIGN TRADE

Trade relations between China and the rest of the world are of exceptional magnitude. A Chinese particularity in international trade is their special choice of business partner. China has not only maintained trade relations with the global players, i.e. the greatest economies of the world, but has also engaged in closely-knit trade relations with African and South-east Asian countries. Their choice of trade partner tends to fluctuate a great deal. The People's Republic does not like to commit itself to long-term agreements, leading to a quick turnover of international partners. The reasons for this could also be political in nature.

In 2017, the three largest and most important trade partners in relation to import and export were the United States, the European Union and Japan. They lay a great deal of value in their trade relationships with south and east Asia. Among the top 20 trade partners in China during 2017 were Japan, Hongkong (NB: Hongkong is listed as an autonomous region of China in the list of international trade partners), South Korea, Taiwan (NB – see Hongkong), Vietnam, Malaysia, India,

Thailand, Singapore, Indonesia and the Philippines, a total of eleven states in this cultural area. They also have far-reaching trade relations with Brazil and South Africa, as well as Saudi Arabia and the United Arab Emirates in the Middle East.

EXCURSUS: THE (NEW) SILK ROAD

The "One Belt, One Road" project is often referred to as the "New Silk Road" in German-speaking countries. Its aim is to create a new trade network and a common infrastructure with more than 60 trade partners. The "old" silk road was the description of the old trade routes between China and Europe, which Marco Polo described. In the new silk road, they hope to develop new land and sea routes inside this historic corridor. Countries in Asia, Africa and Europe, in particular, should benefit greatly from it. Many countries are participating but others are sceptical about the project, particularly in consideration of their own commercial opportunities. Germany has, for example, signed the Memorandum of Foundation, while Japan and the United States are unwilling to take part. There is also loud criticism here that China has put economically weaker participants at risk, by giving them financial loans for infrastructure projects, which could make them dependent upon China for the foreseeable future.

A large proportion of Chinese imports are industrial goods from the high-tech sector and industrial machinery. The largest part of these imports come from Japan and the United States. The most popular exports are electronic devices, textiles, agricultural products and chemicals. Trade takes place to a large extent by sea. Three of the five most congested ports in the world can be found in China.

Even though Russia is much further back in the list of trade partners, it is linked by a significant trade network. China exports mainly electronics, textiles and shoes to Russia. In return it imports energy resources from Russia, such as crude oil. The intention is to increase the trade volume in this area. At the moment, there are several pipeline projects being planned or have been put into operation. This should reduce the traffic on the railways as the main bulk of the crude oil is presently being carried on rail tankers. Recently electricity is also being exported by Russia to China.

In recent decades the growing number of foreign investments made by China has become a significant characteristic in its globalisation. Since 2005, Chinese companies have been expanding and investing in developing countries. Worldwide, around 90 million US Dollars were invested in foreign companies during 2013. China sees great potential in European countries and is increasingly investing capital in them, particularly in Germany. There are a number of reasons for this. Chinese companies often buy foreign companies, or at least try to merger with them, in order to bring goods, often well-known tradenames, to the Chinese domestic market. Often, domestic political hurdles are given as the reason for this as, despite the opening-up of the market economy, high taxes or quota regulations are great obstacles towards the economic growth of Chinese companies. Companies in countries with liberal market economies can side-step these obstacles and difficulties, such as the possibility to export, are eased. On Chinese soil, the regulatory measures, imposed on the marketing of goods by the government are fraught with barriers. In addition to the examples given above, there is a large number of Chinese investment and merger models for foreign investments. The main thing which connects them is the prospect of a quick profit. Not all projects are successful. Chinese investors often underestimate the situation in foreign market economies. A good example of this was the plan of a Chinese car manufacturer. In 2004, the concern bought almost 49% of the shares in a South Korean car manufacturer for around 500 million US Dollars. The plan was to produce a new sport utility vehicle for the Chinese market. In order to make the production profitable, the company attempted to reduce the wages of the workers. Their plans were blocked by the South Korean union. The new car model was never made. As the economic crisis of 2008 hit the Chinese economy, the investors in the South Korean automobile company had to dispose of their shares resulting in a loss of 500 million US Dollars.

EXCURSUS: LOST IN TRANSLATION

In general, the values of the Chinese system do not seem compatible with those of America and Europe. In an interview with a Chinese newspaper, the vice president of an electronics manufacturer looked back at the cooperation he had with business partners in France. He complained that some decision-making processes were painfully slow. One reason for that was that his French partners were not able to speak Chinese and stubbornly refused to speak to him in English.

In general though, such failures are not expected or usual among Chinese companies. Between the mid-1990s and 2010, Chinese investors were involved in business mergers or takeovers with more than 25,000 foreign companies.

CHINA'S ENERGY INDUSTRY

Energy production in China has risen dramatically since the 1980s. At the same time, the consumption of energy nationally has been rising, leading to an increase in the "energy hunger" of the economy. Improvement in the standard of living of the people has contributed greatly towards this. The largest proportion of Chinese electricity is generated using fossil fuels. About 80 percent of their total power is from coal, oil and gas. A relatively high proportion of the rest comes from hydropower. 17 percent is generated in great dams, like the Three Gorges Dam. Very little energy comes from nuclear power plants, which counts for only 3 percent of the total consumption.

China possesses a gigantic potential for natural resources, such as coal and oil. One problem for the Chinese economy, however, is its geographic spread. While the northeast is rich in coal and oil, there is great potential in the southwest for the development of energy resources using hydropower. Also, in the northeast part of the country, there are large coal deposits but there are logistical problems which leave the heavily industrial regions of Guangzhou and Shanghai short of power.

In recent years there has been a departure from coal energy, predominantly in order to reduce greenhouse gases. In addition, The People's Republic is attempting to make itself less dependent upon the raw material coal. For these reasons, thousands of coal-run power stations have been closed in recent years. In the future, a balanced energy mix should ensure a more flexible energy economy, although they are not yet aiming for a fully clean form of energy production. Instead their energy is to be won from oil and gas power stations, although they are also looking at sources for renewable energy generation, in particular using hydropower, and plans for extracting energy from Nuclear power stations are being also being expedited. By these means, the generation of power using fossil fuels has been reduced to 60 percent of their total requirements.

In order to guarantee a stable economy, China has been importing large amounts of oil since the early 90s, mostly from the Middle East. Chinese companies have increased their investments in oil fields throughout the world so that they can avoid dependency on a single international partner.

THE CHINESE COAL INDUSTRY

The People's Republic of China is not only the largest producer of coal, but also its largest consumer. As already mentioned, they have been reducing their total consumption of coal for the generation of energy, although in practice, the energy economy is not being converted at the speed that the coal power stations are being closed. Because of this, large amounts of coal have to be imported annually. The main trade partners are Indonesia and Australia. New coal power stations have had to be built to satisfy the needs of the rapidly growing economy. This has the effect that the building of alternative energy sources, such as hydropower or nuclear power only serve to slow down the building of the new coal power stations. In the main, the local governments are responsible for the development of these power sources as part of their self-government rules, but, in the main, they obstinately refuse to close the coal power stations. The local officials do not want to risk losing jobs in their regions. This all leads to the strange situation, noticed by environmental organisations, that there are power stations presently being built which have long been cancelled by the central government in Beijing. Of course, that is not happening in all provinces. The local governments usually try to toe the party line.

China is also involved in building coal power stations in other countries. Environmentalists believe that approximately one quarter of the CO_2 emitted worldwide originated from Chinese coal power stations.

The coal reserves of the People's Republic are gigantic but not infinite. It is thought that about 60 billion tons of hard coal and 50 million tons of brown coal are to be found within the national territory of the People's Republic. In all, these reserves should last for about 30 years, if the rate of mining does not increase further. The total amount of coal production has tripled in the last twenty years.

In China, about half a dozen mining companies are in production, which are producing CO_2 emission at the same rate as that of Germany.

By far the biggest opencast mine can be found in Haerwusu in Inner Mongolia, an autonomous region of China, where around 20 million tons of raw coal are mined every year. A further expansion of the production rate is already in the planning phase. As most of the coal consumers live in the urban areas on the Chinese coast, the transport of coal from Haerwusu regularly causes massive traffic problems on China's highways. As a result, some smaller local mines have been erected, some dating back as far as the 1960s, to alleviate some of the congestion. It seems that their efforts have been successful. About half of the coal mined in China comes from small mines, of which there are many thousands. However, some of these mines have been fraught with problems. Not all the mines were built, adhering to the local government's safety guidelines. The result has been catastrophic mining accidents which have cost thousands of workers' lives. Despite the domestic political challenges, the country's demand for coal is continuing to grow. The main use for the coal is for generating electricity, in second place is the steel industry. Both are established and at the same time growing industrial areas.

The use of coal in the private sector is government regulated. Although coal consumption was once omnipresent, in the rural areas, the trend is now declining. In urban areas, it is hard to find coal being used in domestic ovens, as this was largely strictly forbidden some years ago. Use of coal in the house led to massive health issues because the smoke was not diverted up the chimney but spread into the rooms. The result was the high rate of death following respiratory illnesses. The number of people in China who reportedly died each year from the long-term effects of coal smoke was about 400,000. Another factor was that people cooked over coal fires. Heavy metals contaminated the foods which led to an increase in illnesses, such as laryngeal or oesophagus cancer. Generally, it was considered that the air quality inside the houses at the beginning of the economic upswing was better than that outside. In the meantime, the danger of coal burning has been somewhat mitigated by using chimneys at home. However, this practice has not yet been implemented everywhere.

CHINA'S CRUDE OIL AND GAS

Like so many other branches of the economy in China, the crude oil industry is growing rapidly. However, in this energy sector, the same problems are being experienced as with the coal industry. The consumption of crude oil is growing and cannot be covered by domestic production, forcing China to import large amounts of it, even though the People's Republic itself has a large amount of untapped oil deposits. At the end of the 1960s, gigantic resources were discovered in the Songhua Jiang-Liao basin among other places. The most important discovery was the Daqing oilfield in the province of Heilongjiang in northern China. In those days, China was preparing to become a great exporter and until the mid-80s, almost 20 million tons of crude oil were exported, particularly to Japan. In 1993, domestic consumption exceeded all China's production resources for the first time and China was not able to meet its own domestic requirements. Since then, China itself has become the greatest importer of this commodity in the world. In 2013, China imported more oil than the leading country at the time, the United States.

The Chinese government found itself in great distress due to the oil production not being able to meet the consumption of its people. To solve the problem, the three biggest oil companies in China (the China National Offshore Oil Corporation, the China National Petroleum Corporation and Sinopec) invested in the development of oilfields abroad. Their main investments were oilfields in countries which could provide large amounts of oil but which did not have the economic means to extract the crude oil. Agreements were made for cooperation with Indonesia and Malaysia. There is also some cooperation with Australia. The People's Republic of China possesses one of the world's biggest strategic oil reserves, which the government has been investing in massively since 2004. With the establishment of the oil reserve, the government wanted to make China's energy economy less dependent on oil imports. In China there are three such crude oil reserves, which were all constructed on the coast. There are no reliable reports as to how much oil can be collected in these three reservoirs, but foreign observers estimate the total amount of oil stored to be about 500 million barrels. In comparison with the other worldwide largest reserves, China takes third place with this estimate. The only countries who can exceed the size of the Chinese oil reserves are the those of the United States and Japan.

Being the third most important energy source after coal and oil, natural gas has earned a valuable place in the Chinese energy economy. There are plans to expand the production of electricity from gas power and, according to the government, they intend to replace some of the existing coal power stations with it. It is known that China also owns some strategic oil reserves similar to those of crude oil, although little is known about the volumes involved. It is apparent that their natural gas reserves are supplied from their own production and around half of the natural gas reserves come from the Sichuan province.

GOLD, ORES, METALS UND MORE

Nearly every province in China has its own reserves of iron ore, their value to the economy being very mixed. Important mining areas can be found in the provinces of Guangdong, Gansu, Guizhou and south Sichuan. The ores which are mined there are mostly for local use and are delivered to the iron and steel works close by. Other important natural resources, which are available in large amounts are manganese, lead, zinc, tin and gold. In China there are also large amounts of bauxite and the world's largest deposits of antimony. In addition, a significant industry has built up around the mining of minerals. Salt extraction from evaporation plants on the Chinese coast has become increasingly important and inland there are also many gigantic salt fields from which huge amounts of minerals are extracted. Iron pyrites, fluorite, gypsum and limestone have also been found.

A very large part of the Chinese mining industry is involved in the extraction of gold ore. In recent times, China has become the largest gold producer in the world and in 2006, overtook the previous leader, South Africa, which had held that title since 1905. In 2019,

China produced about 300 tons of gold. The simple reason for the change of leader was that the South Africans halved their gold production and the Chinese doubled theirs. It was only possible to double the Chinese production due to foreign investors, who come mainly from Canada, Australia and India.

Today, the China National Gold Group Corporation (CNGGC) is the most important of the approximately 2000 Chinese companies who are active in the gold processing industry. The CNGGC is responsible for about 20 percent of China's total gold production. It is the only company which has ventured into the stock market; the other gold producers are relatively unimportant in the global market. Most Chinese gold is not exported, but used for the manufacture of jewellery and other valuable objects. Over the last few years, Chinese high society has dramatically increased its demand for gold. Chinese companies are also making foreign investments and in this respect are roughly following the same political course that they have with their offshore oil. Significant investments were made above all in Africa. In 2015, there were almost 120 mining projects in African countries, which belonged to the Chinese. They are not only interested in gold, but also other metals and minerals. In Namibia, for example, a Chinese company, the China General Nuclear Power Corporation, is involved in the mining of the worldwide biggest deposits of uranium.

Even though China is the world leader in gold production, the gold reserves of the country are comparatively small. It is estimated that only 7 percent of the world's gold reserves belong to China.

RARE EARTH IN CHINA

The Chinese national economy is not only at the forefront in gold and ores, but also with the element group of rare earths. These days, seemingly unimportant elements, such as promethium and neodymium are of great significance. Without rare earth, none of our smart phones or plasma screen would work, nor any electric engine. In medicine, rare earth is used in radiology as a component of contrast media. These "rare earths" are not really rare at all, which causes some confusion. Rare earth is quite common and can be found in many places. Rare earth is not found in deposits like seams of coal. However, they are irreplaceable due to the world's hunger for technology and therefore extremely sought-after. China has taken full advantage of this opportunity. By far the world's biggest deposit of rare earth can be found in Inner Mongolia. Around 71 percent of the world's rare earth for industrial use is extracted in China, for example in the well-known Bayan-Obo Mine. China wants to exploit this fact and it plays a big role in the economic conflict with the USA.

Despite the immense demand for world trade, production of rare earth has fallen recently in China. This is due to the extreme costs of extraction. Because of the economic differences with the USA, exports to that country have diminished. This has the advantage that the People's Republic of China has been able to meet its own needs in the electronic branch, a fact which is not the case with other raw materials.

CHINA AS "CHEAP" COUNTRY?

For decades China was known as a "cheap" country. Goods, such as gym shoes, handbags and t-shirts boasted the label "Made in China". While the label "Made in Germany" even today promises quality, this did not apply to Chinese products. Items from the far east were considered junk-goods, and the fact that as Chinese (textile) products often bore the names of renowned western manufacturers but were made under inhumane conditions in mega-factories, showed the People's Republic in a bad light for which they received much bad press. One of the reasons why these products were criticised was that they were mostly bought on the internet and arrived directly at the consumer's door – often for just a few pence. The importance of cheap consumer goods has been in decline recently, but still remains a relatively large part of the Chinese economy, being almost 50 percent of the gross national product of the country. In the meantime, China's industry has caught up with the top producers in the automobile segment, telecommunication and the arms industry. Chinese products, made in their own country, have become well established in the European, Asian and North

American markets. However, an important factor in their success has been the shift of the production plants of western companies to China. This saves European and American companies a lot of money: Productions costs in the People's Republic are far lower than those in Germany, also the purchase price of raw materials in many segments is much lower due to the short delivery routes. This is an absolute gain for the Chinese government and those employees working in the factories of foreign investors also profit financially compared to those working in Chinese production plants.

The Chinese industry itself is very diverse. One important segment includes the iron and steel industry, aluminium production and the extraction of crude oil. The production of fertilisers, textiles and clothing, cement, shoes, toys and communication technology are also significant sectors. China has also established itself on the world market with its automotive industry. However, production is not only confined to cars and heavy goods vehicles. In China, railway vehicles and ships are also produced in great numbers.

No other economic branch is growing quicker in China than the industrial sector. Annually growth is said to be around 10 percent. There has also been a significant trend towards privatisation of companies. This is also true of the smaller sectors. However, the most important mainstay of Chinese industry, the production of steel, remains in state possession.

EXCURSUS: AN EYE FOR AN EYE - THE TRADE WAR BETWEEN THE USA AND CHINA

Donald Trump has a big problem with the growing economy of China. The reason for the American president's annoyance is the trade deficit between the USA and the People's Republic. The USA's exports of goods to China amount to approximately 130 billion US Dollars, whereas the reciprocal value of goods exported by China to the USA accounts for about 505 billion US Dollars. Trump retaliated by imposing punitive tariffs, at first on washing machines and solar panels, followed by steel and aluminium goods. And that was only the start of a cascade of punitive measures. About 1,300 Chinese products were affected by tariffs during 2018.

The People's Republic retaliated by imposing tariffs on aluminium, steel and a further 100 products "Made in USA". These tariffs included a variety of products, such as soy beans and even aeroplanes. A series of retaliations followed on both sides, with the result that tariffs were being imposed of up to 25 percent. There does not seem to be an end in sight, to the disappointment of the global economic market. Sometimes, these measures interrupt the delivery chains and even foreign companies with production sites in USA are suffering as a result. As an example, German car manufacturers are among those disadvantaged by the situation.

CHINA'S STEEL

In 2018, China's government announced a great accomplishment. The People's Republic had established itself as the world's largest steel manufacturer. More than 50 percent of the world's steel was being produced in China, a total of almost 930 million tons. The country is the most significant steel producer by far in the world. Six of the ten largest producers worldwide have their headquarters in China. In 2008, only half of that amount was being produced. Due to the economic growth of the country, they needed more raw materials. Even though China is rich in iron ore, the country's resources are not sufficient to cover their own requirements for the steel industry. Similar to the situation with the oil and coal industries, China has been importing iron ore since the start of the millennium to cover its needs. Exports and high debt repayments are causing constant erosion to the profit margins in the steel industry.

AUTOMOBILES FOR THE WORLD MARKET

China is the world's largest market for automobiles. In 2018, the Chinese produced significantly more cars (27 million) than the USA (11.3 million) and Japan (8.7 million). Germany's car manufacturing figures are small in comparison, with 4.7 million automobiles being produced in 2019. As far back as 2010, China was producing more cars than the USA and Japan together. The demand has remained unchanged: Chinese cars are as popular as ever. Due to the rise in average Chinese income, more and more people are able to buy their own car. This factor has allowed production and turnover figures to remain at a constant level. In the meantime, most of the cars they make are sold within China. Chinese manufacturers have been successfully exporting completed cars and spare parts for the last twenty years.

Nearly all internationally significant automobile producers are involved in joint ventures in China, although the Chinese government only allows a maximum of two foreign investors to be involved in each company. This is also true for German automobile manufacturers, such as BMW, Mercedes Benz and

Volkswagen, all of which are active in China. However, recently a few international car manufacturers have withdrawn from this market, giving such reasons as worries over becoming too dependent on the Chinese market and economic-political tensions. Parallel to this, there are dozens of purely Chinese automobile manufacturers whose models and trademarks are almost unknown in our western culture. The trend is growing; it can be assumed that the Chinese automobile market will continue to grow in order to satisfy the national and international demand.

China's pioneering role is not only limited to the automobile market, using traditional combustion engines. The country is the worldwide largest producer of e-cars. In 2018, 1.8 million electric cars were produced. Their main consumers are from within their own country, 96 percent of e-cars presently on the Chinese streets are from their own production sites. In today's industrial landscape, there are expectations of a vast amount of e-car production and significant growth of this market owing to an increase in environmental awareness.

EXCURSUS: DRIVING IN THE FAR EAST

Any German who wants to drive a car in China must first go through a long process to obtain a licence, as driving in the streets of China is only permitted if you are in possession of a Chinese driving licence. Contrary to many other countries, German and international driving licences are not accepted. Ignoring the law leads to draconian punishment: In the worst case, even expulsion. However, it is possible to obtain a temporary driving licence for short visits. If the trip to China is expected to take a bit longer, it is necessary to go through a lengthy procedure, involving the procurement of much document-tation, and a driving test. Papers required include identification confirmation, including copies, a certificate of health, several photos, the German driving licence and translations of all of those documents. After theory training and practical driving lessons, it is necessary to pass a test on the computer. The content often involves a response to specific situations in Chinese traffic. The test is made even harder by the fact that the test is only available in Chinese or extremely bad English.

BANKS AND EQUITY TRADING

By far the biggest number of Chinese banks belong to the state. The national bank is the People's Bank of China (PBC). Financial control of the bank system is maintained by the Finance Ministry, which in turn is under the direction of the State Council. The PBC has a variety of duties. For example, it issues the Renminbi and administers the accounts of the government and its organisations. In addition, the PBC directs China's international trade. There is also a number of banks which take care of the economic sectors of specific branches, such as the agricultural bank, which only deal with farming business transactions. The most important bank for the Chinese people is the Industrial and Commercial Bank of China (ICBC), which deals with normal everyday business and is similar to a savings bank.

The significance of the banks generally grew after wide-ranging economic reform in China. It is now possible, at least in theory, for companies and private citizens to be able to access loans outside the normal state funding. This is very important, particularly for traders.

About 75 percent of the state loans are given to state companies. The state is also increasingly borrowing money. Lenders are often foreign organisations, associations and other countries. The People's Republic has also obtained loans from the World Bank, the United Nations and Japan.

There are two big stock markets in China – the Shanghai Stock Exchange and the Shenzhen Stock Exchange. Together, they make up the biggest stock market in the world. The Chinese stock index, CSI 300 contains about 300 publicly listed companies.

PROJECTS FOR THE FUTURE OF CHINA

The gap between rich and poor is huge. The Chinese government is attempting to reduce this divide with various projects, particularly benefitting the regions in the west, north-east, south-west and central China. The main effort is in the building of new gas pipelines, electricity conduits and water pipelines to enable all the people to be supplied.

The water supply is particularly important. Rural regions are still not connected to the national water grid and there are recurring shortages of water supply in the urban areas. The connection to the fresh water and sewerage networks is not the main problem. The uneven distribution of water is something which causes great concern to the Chinese government. There is not enough water in some regions. A more just and balanced distribution is one of the main discussion points for future reforms.

Water management is a very important subject in China. The number of people who did not have access to a groundwater well in 2015 was 63 million. This number includes many Chinese people who have access to water but that the quality of the water could not be described as fresh water. The contamination of the drinking water with sewerage is a very serious problem, which causes large amounts of the population to have diarrhoeal diseases. An analysis by UNICEF found that more than 10 percent of Chinese drinking water was badly contaminated with microorganisms. Generally, drinking tap water is not advised. However, for the general population, there is often no alternative.

The extremely rapid economic development of the country has led to an additional burden on its water resources. Nearly 60 percent of Chinese cities suffer from water shortages independent of the season or amount of rainfall. 15 percent of those cities suffer from significant water shortages throughout the year. Around 325 million people had no access to sanitary facilities in 2015, according to estimates, only 52 percent of sewerage is processed through treatment plants. Instead of having sanitary facilities similar to those of the west, so-called "composting toilets" are not uncommon. The availability of toilets is also subject to the gap between rich and poor and between urban and rural communities.

Apart from the shortage of water, the gigantic economic growth of China brings other problems with it. The country is suffering from massive environmental pollution. The government has recognised this and has ordered numerous initiatives and regulations to be put in place.

The reclamation of land is intruding greatly on the habitat of animals and plants. This is particularly noticeable in the coastal regions where the land has had to make way for industry, aquaculture and agricultural operations. 65% of the Yellow River area of the Chinese coast is reported to be totally destroyed. Another problem is desertification, meaning the formation of new deserts. In western China, this has become a serious threat. Already well over a third of the region is considered to be desert, which is constantly growing. An example of this is the Gobi Desert, which expands by about 2,500 square kilometres per year. The reason for this is said to be overgrazing and the flourishing economy, which requires increasing amounts of water. In order to stop the widescale desertification, the Chinese developed a project called "Green Wall of China" with the aim of planting a 5,000-kilometre-long belt of forest in the desert area. In total, more than 35,000 kilometres of forest is to be planted at a cost of some eight billion US Dollars. The "Green Wall" is said to be one of the most ambitious ecological projects of the present day. Despite this, there is significant criticism, stating that, although they praise the investments made, there are better methods to counter the growth of the desert. The Chinese do not share those doubts. The government intends not only to prevent further desertification but also to create green land in the areas which have already become desert. They believe that they can completely cover the desert lands with forest by the year 2050. Some believe that China has set a good example by making plans for a "Green Wall". In Africa, they too are planning such a "Green Wall". Many African states south of the Sahara have got together to plant the "Green Wall of Africa", which is designed to counteract the expansion of the Sahara.

CHINA AND CLIMATE CHANGE

Climatic changes have had a significant effect on China's economy, society and environment. These effects are already quantifiable: In comparison to the previous century, the mean temperature and the mean precipitation rate has increased. These trends are set to continue. Sea levels are rising constantly and the glaciers are receding. The former is a serious problem for the People's Republic, because the coastal regions, those which lie the lowest, are the regions which have the highest density of population. Several of China's megacities such as Shanghai, Tianjin and Guangzhou, which are also important economic areas, are endangered by a rise in the sea level. Droughts and floods are also becoming more frequent, all events which effect the rural areas most. A rise in poverty follows a crop failure. The Chinese forests are suffering from similar climate change problems as those in Europe and Germany. The lack of rainfall causes the number of pests to increase significantly, causing irreparable damage to the trees. There is also an expectancy that the conditions following climate changes would cause an increase in sickness rates. In some areas, there is a risk that there could be a 50 percent increase in the infection rate of malaria. Within the Chinese population and their government, there is a general understanding that climate change is a fact – an understanding which is not always accepted outside of western democracies. Surveys have confirmed this. The majority of the Chinese population agree that it is necessary to actively work towards fulfilling the targets set by at the Paris Climate Treaty. There is general agreement that the climate change is largely due to human causes and that air pollution plays a big role in that situation. The people of China agree that their individual solutions to the problems of climate change are particularly promising. Public opinion is that the Chinese government's programme for the reduction of greenhouse gases is effective. This is also helped by the fact that most Chinese people believe that their government know what they are doing, partly due to their experience with tax and economic politics, which have been regarded as successful.

The Chinese government has only recently become active in combating the challenges of climate change. The central government in Beijing has published regulations with regard to CO_2 emissions, which are implemented in different ways by different regions. This does not mean that they are carried out in a truly consistent way. Their decentralised form of administration means that the administration is left to the officials at the local and provincial level, whether the regulations are carried out. Local politicians decided for themselves whether they believe that the improvement of the climate is worth the disadvantages towards the economy. If this is the case, climate protection is normally not the highest priority. China believes that they are only "partly to blame" as they are in the process of building up their industrialisation, whereas other countries have completed theirs. So, although the Chinese government supports the efforts of the international community towards protecting the climate, they are not unified in their approach to it. This results in the fact that they have reduced their CO_2 emissions at a lower rate than other industrial countries. The fact that climate change is taken seriously by Chinese politics was shown by the reaction of the government, in 2017, as the USA pulled out of the Paris Climate Treaty. China called on the governments of the other member states to stop USA from pulling out and to continue working towards the agreed climate goals.

As far back as 2013, the government published a strategy paper on reducing the effects of climate change. A part of that dealt with the recycling of rainwater, which involved the collection of rainwater in special plants in order to reduce the danger of flooding. Air quality was also to be improved and the Chinese government has had some success in reducing smog. Measures are to include the improvement of air quality and a reduction in the use of coal. There is a whole list of measures in that respect. Each province is responsible for actively fighting climate change. For example, as in Germany, old-fashioned light bulbs have been substituted for energy-saving ones. In some provinces, the capture of sun energy using solar energy systems has been introduced, although this does not apply to all. Solar energy is mainly used for the heating of buildings.

China's part in the fight against climate change is becoming increasingly significant, because of the size of its industry and it becoming the largest economy in the world.

EXCURSUS: EMISSION FREE ENERGY VS. ECO-LOGY

The impressive Three Gorges Dam can be found in Sandouping near the city of Yichang. It is the biggest hydroelectric power plant in the world with a capacity of 22.5 gigawatts, and it is an important energy producer and one of the most controversial projects ever. Environmentalists protested against the building of the dam, which started in 1998. The existence of thousands of animals and plants has been threatened and the people have suffered too. The flooding of the area caused countless people to have to leave home and whole cities sank in the man-made floods. The building was also accompanied by immense corruption. In addition, the hydro-electric power station was built in the middle of a seismically active zone: If the dam were to break, the lives of 15 million people would be threatened. According to the officials, the dam is stable enough to withstand earthquakes of up to 7 on the Richter scale.

THE CHINESE TAX SYSTEM

Taxes are the largest source of income in the Chinese state. A series of reforms were necessary in order to ensure that a modern tax system could be put in place. In 1994, the People's Republic established a tax system based on a socialist market economy. Also in China, the Finance Ministry is the official authority for tax policies.

In China, there are a number of different taxes, some of which may sound familiar to the western ear but some may not. (Note: The names of the tax reforms in China do not always make sense in translation. Therefore, the following list describes a general sense of the content).

Sales Tax:
The Chinese sales tax includes three different types of tax: The value added tax, the trade tax and the excise tax.

Income Tax:
Income tax in China includes corporation tax and the individual income of citizens who use the operating profits of companies to benefit individuals.

Resource Tax:

Resource tax is paid by people who use natural resources in order to make financial profits.

Taxes for Special Purposes:

Many types of taxes fall under this category, for example city maintenance taxes, farmland taxes, property tax or the tax payable for investments in fixed assets.

Behaviour Tax:

This could include, for example, the use of automobiles and ships, stamp duty on property purchases or document taxes.

Agricultural Tax:

This group includes taxes for keeping animals, or animal use as well as agricultural taxes as such.

An important tax income is one of custom duties.

The above-mentioned taxes are for Chinese citizens. Foreign investors and companies only have to pay part of these taxes at present. In total there are 14 different types of taxes for foreigners. These are: value added tax, special income tax on companies where the profits flow out of the country and foreign companies generally, income tax, resource tax, property tax, automobile use and registration tax, stamp duty, document tax, "slaughter tax", agricultural tax and custom duties.

This form of taxing foreign investors is also paid by the special regions of Macau, Taiwan and Hongkong. The same applies to Chinese citizens with their places of residence outside of China.

CHINA AS A SERVICE-ORIENTATED COUNTRY

The service sector in China is growing rapidly and, parallel to the manufacturing sector, is fast becoming one of the most important financial mainstays of the country. One of the main reasons for the boom in the service industry is opening of the markets to national and international investors. There has been enormous growth in both the wholesale and retail sectors. Shopping malls, like those in the USA, and restaurant and hotel chains have been established.

CHINA AS A HOLIDAY DESTINATION?

The increasing prosperity and the establishment of a Chinese middle class, which for the first time was able to afford to travel, has caused a strong growth in the tourist industry. The Chinese people like to travel these days and do so in great numbers. In purely mathematical terms, every fifth tourist is a Chinese citizen. Long-distance travel is particularly popular and tourist experts see the trend growing rapidly. Even though the various reforms have relaxed the restrictions on travel over recent years, there is still are great number of official hurdles which need to be overcome. It is believed that only about seven percent of all Chinese are in possession of a passport.

The popularity of China as a tourist destination has increased over the past few years. In 2015, China became the fourth most popular destination in the world behind France, the USA and Spain. In the meantime, tourism has become a significant source of income. The share of tourism in the gross national product in 2017 is estimated at more than 11 percent. The World Tourism Organisation of the UNO (UNWTO) estimates that China's share of international tourism during 2020 will exceed 8.6 percent of the total world market.

There is no other state in the world which enjoys business tourism as much as China. In no other country do companies send their representatives abroad so much. In 2012, Chinese companies spent almost 200 billion US Dollars on business trips. This also makes China top of the charts in this respect.

TELECOMMUNICATION AND THE INTERNET

The three manufacturers which dominate the Chinese telecommunications market are China Unicom, China Telecom and China Mobil. Landlines are not as popular in that country as they are in Europe. Only 15 percent of the population own a telephone connected to a landline. Mobile communication is much more popular. Roughly 1.1 billion Chinese own a mobile phone. All the above-mentioned companies own a 3G licence and are, at least in theory, capable of good network coverage.

The country's own producers of smartphones are not the top choice of the Chinese public, who prefer European or north American brands. Manufacturers, such as Nokia, Samsung, Apple and Motorola are most popular in China. Well known Chinese manufacturers, such as Huawei are more dependent upon sales to Africa, south America and southeast Asia for their turnover. In these countries, the market is growing rapidly in general, but for Huawei in particular.

Chinese network providers offer a range of communications services with their products and these are either paid for using a pre-paid card or through monthly payments after completion of a contract. They rely upon DSL technologies and WLAN for internet connections. In addition, fibreglass techno-logy is widespread. China is the second largest internet user in the world.

CHINA'S DESIRE FOR LUXURY

As with the tourism branch and the automobile industry, China's desire for all kinds of luxury goods is growing. Their increasing income means that they can afford to buy more and their demand for status symbols has increased significantly. About a quarter of all worldwide consumers of luxury goods is Chinese and the trend is growing sharply. Basically, in China the target group is different. While luxury goods in Europe and north America are usually bought by people over 40 years, in China the demand lies more with the younger people, with the main demand for luxury goods being with consumers of between 18 and 50. According to market analyses, about 80 percent of luxury articles are bought by people who have not yet reached their 45th birthday. As already mentioned, the consumption and possession of such articles is seen as a status symbol. It is then not surprising that manufacturers offer those goods which are easily visible, such as trademarks like Louis Vuitton, Chanel and Gucci, as well as expensive watches. Branches of Rolex, Cartier, Breitling and Omega are numerous in China's large cities. Apart from watches and clothes, handbags, jewellery, shoes and perfumes are in high demand.

EXCURSUS: A BIT OF LUXURY FOR GOOD FRIENDS

The giving of luxury gifts was normal practice in government circles and was considered to be so widespread that the government found it necessary to forbid them in a bid to fight corruption. The ban was put into practice in October 2012 and made a considerable dent in the national market: For the first time in more recent history the turnover of luxury goods reduced slightly during 4th Quarter of 2012. The reduction was most noticeable in the watch market. The giving of expensive watches from reputable European manufacturers was seen as a cliché for corruption in government circles. However, the intervention of the state did not cause long-term negative consequences for the luxury market. In the following years, it became noticeable that Chinese returning from holidays or business trips to Europe or the United States brought back large amounts of such products.

The Chinese love luxury cars, particularly German ones. The Chinese luxury market has been dominated by Audi, as market leader, for more than 20 years. Their most significant competitors are also German (Mercedes Benz and BMW) who were able to enter the Chinese market with new concepts. In 2004, two of every three luxury cars in China were manufactured in the Audi factory, although this is slowly diminishing. In 2009, the market share sank to 42 percent. However, the trademark Audi remains the dominating force in China. The first choice for the Chinese state fleet continues to be the manufacturer from Ingolstadt. Some of the models are designed specifically for the Chinese market. BMW has also adjusted its models to cater for the Chinese and European market individually and made a model specifically for Chinese government officials, which offered more space for the front passenger.

CORRUPTION, CYBERCRIME AND HYPERBOLE

When China issues statistics about its economy, demography or other developments, these should always be treated with some scepticism. The officials and administrators often publish estimates and this is one of the reasons why the population figures are often based on projections. Critics believe that the figures issued on the total population of the People's Republic could range anywhere between +/- 100 million people. Such inaccuracies have an influence on the income per person calculations, causing the total picture in China to be somewhat fuzzy. The companies within China also do not always share their real figures, particular when it comes to their turnover. There have been cases where companies have artificially raised their turnover figures by up to 40 percent. This form of swindle can cause outsiders to feel unsure about the true situation in China.

The flourishing economy in China is also a flourishing place for cybercrime, which has been increasing dramatically since 2016. Chinese officials were able to trace around 90,000 people who were actively participating in black market activities online. This caused an increase in the surveillance of suspects and their activities in the internet.

EXCURSUS: THE HUNT FOR VIRTUAL GOLD

China's prosperity led to the increase in people spending their time on video games online on their PCs. Roleplay was particularly popular and this led to the formation of the branch which hardly exists in western countries: Professional online players participate in "Gold Farming". Several dozen players sit together in offices and generate virtual currency or valuable game material, which can be sold for real money. It is the dream job of many a young Chinese and happens to be illegal. The developers of such games have been trying to put an end to this activity for years. After all, they are spoiling the fun for other, fairer players. Even though "gaming for money" sounds like the ideal job, the working conditions are more than bad. Twelve-hour shifts are not uncommon and no breaks are allowed. The players sleep in the same room that they work in. There is also some evidence of deaths occurring.

Corruption is not a new phenomenon in the history of China. For just as long there have been punishments for them, dating back to the early Imperial Era. Today, corruption is also widespread: According to a registered anti-corruption agency called Transparency International, China takes the 79th place out of 176 countries which were sampled for the most corruption in the Asian region. The all-powerful Communist Party, which operates without controlling bodies, provides the perfect conditions for excessive corruption. The most 'popular' offences include the illegal acquisition of state property, embezzlement and bribery of politicians. The negative effect of that is the increasing mistrust of the population towards the government, waste of financial and other resources and general destabilisation of the political system. State Leader, Xi Jinping, initiated a large anti-corruption campaign, where dozens of sometimes high-ranking party members of the CPC were ousted from their positions and convicted. However, the population remains sceptical that these measures were effective. Convictions are seldom in this respect, particularly because they must be sanctioned by other party organisations and that does not happen very often. That means that the real danger of a conviction remains very low. This, in turn, results in more corruption being encouraged.

The organisation "Reporters Without Borders" listed China in last place in the worldwide index for freedom of the press. Censuring in the People's Republic is very restrictive, particularly in respect of the internet. Social media platforms, such as Facebook, Twitter and YouTube are generally not accessible for normal citizens. Instead, the state offers alternatives, such as messenger services. The use of search machines, like Google, is also restricted. Searches which are not acceptable to the party are filtered out. These measures in total are known as the "Great Firewall of China".

Newspapers also suffer the same censuring fate. It is said that editors receive a daily briefing from the state about what they can report. In 2009, newspaper articles regarding the 20th anniversary of the massacre at Tiananmen Square were deleted from foreign newspapers. In 2011, the two private newspapers, "Beijing News" and "Beijing Times", were put under the control of the state. The aim was obviously to guarantee that articles appeared in these newspapers which resembled more the ideology of the state.

CCTV, is the Chinese state television network. All other TV channels in the country are duty-bound to broadcast news programmes from the CCTV. Foreign broadcasting stations are also censured as they find necessary. If the state sees a programme which it finds uncomfortable, they may find it necessary to disturb the signal. This can be done using special satellites, and often takes place during reports which the state leaders consider "precarious". Unwanted content could include, for example, a programme about the Dalai-Lama or the unrest in Tibet. Broadcast stations such as CNN or BBC are not freely available. The installation of satellite dishes which can receive TV programmes from foreign channels is forbidden to the normal citizen. There are a few exceptions, such as in diplomatic circles or hotels.

The above also applies to foreign films. It is possible that scenes with Chinese actors are cut out of the film if it is considered that the content is portrayed in a negative way. This applies, for example to entertain-ment movies from Hollywood where a "bad guy" is played by a Chinese actor, or an actor with Chinese roots. Sexual content is also cut out. If it is not possible to cut the offending scenes out, without completely destroying the sense of the film, the film will be forbidden. Some film producers in Hollywood do not even bother to hand their films over to the censorship officials and so forego the publications of the film in China.

Generally, the attempts at censorship in China seem peculiar to us. In 2008 the Chinese government announced that it would forbid all films which contained monsters, ghosts or demons. This was intended to protect the general public. However, the result was a bustling black-market industry which dealt with pirated copies of the original film which most Chinese were able to see (illegally).

Book publishers are also controlled closely, which has led to the establishment of an "underground pub-lishing" scene, where books can escape censorship. The numbers are enormous. It is estimated that about 60 percent of the books circulating in China come from illegal book publishers. The Chinese government considers them to be "intellectual contamination".

Importing books or magazines which are thought to be harmful for the society is forbidden.

On a smaller scale, censorship is also carried out on music albums and video games. Some tracks have even been completely forbidden.

- Chapter 5 -

CHINA'S MILITARY FORCES

THE PEOPLE'S LIBERATION ARMY

The People's Liberation Army is the biggest army in the world, costing China's government more than 200 million US Dollars per year. Its size is gigantic: 2.2 million soldiers are in active military service and there are a further 1.4 million reservists, which can be called up for service when needed. The Supreme Commander of the army is the chairman of the Central Military Commission, who also happens to be the head of government: Xi Jinping. The People's Liberation Army, or PLA for short, is divided into six parts.

The army, meaning the land forces, is the largest military group in China with 1.6 million active soldiers. The army is divided into 18 groups and an estimated 6,700 tanks and double that amount of artillery pieces. One disadvantage is that despite the large numbers of people, materials and technical equipment is outdated and no longer suitable for its purpose. This should also confirm the role of the People's Liberation Army as a defence army.

215,000 soldiers belong to the navy. The Chinese navy owns dozens over ships and submarines, including two aircraft carriers, eight atomic submarines and five submarines which can carry ballistic rockets. There is a general preference for submarines, which make up the main part of the Chinese fleet.

The air force owns 1,800 fighter planes and about 300 transport machines as well as some reconnaissance aircraft. The air force has about 390,000 soldiers at its disposal.

A new part of the military forces is the strategic support group whom, among other things, is tasked with maintaining communications during military operations and is responsible for the testing of new technology. Several aspects of modern warfare are gathered together in this group of the PLA, including military aerospace.

Another part of the military forces is the support group, which is responsible for medical services, buildings, provisions and transport.

There has been a great deal of interest in the so-called rocket group, which are also known as the second artillery. China is a nuclear power and owns ballistic intercontinental rockets which are capable of targeting almost any part of the earth. Some of the intercontinental rockets, called CSS 4, are capable of hitting any point of land on earth except for south America and a small part of Africa. In addition, they have a large arsenal of short and medium-range rockets. A number of tests on new models are being carried out at present, provoking global protests.

CHINA AS A NUCLEAR POWER

Since 1964, China has officially been a nuclear power and therefore is in possession of a number of operational nuclear weapons. In the same year, the People's Republic declared its intention not to be the first to use nuclear weapons in a conflict. This declaration has been renewed many times over the years and the Chinese repeatedly state their support for nuclear disarmament. According to estimates by military experts, China has an arsenal of 130 operational nuclear warheads.

CONCLUSION

The Author, Paul Krugman, said after a journey to China: "I have seen the future and it will not work". Many people have reached the conclusion that Krugman is right in his assumptions. Many aspects of the economic growth in China seem to be a temporary compromise and an overexploitation of its own country. It is certainly experiencing the effects of its efforts: China is the world champion in exports, a situation which has developed over a very short time. One example is the mining of coal. While 347 million tons were mined in the 1970s, it was a proud 3,600 million tons in 2013. Trend: sinking. Even though the production quotas are still gigantic, the mining has already dropped by 500 million tons of hard coal. Coal power stations are being built which will still not produce enough for the needs of the people. Alternative energy forms are intended to protect the environment but only serve to slow down the building of new coal power stations. The People's Republic is dependent upon imports to drive its economy and to stay the world champions in export. Its competitor, the USA, is developing in the same way as China; mining production figures are sinking. In addition, India is waiting for its chance to become a global player in this respect.

The problem is quickly explained. China's power is built on resources which are not infinite. Although this generates a good cashflow at present, and enables projects, such as the new silk road to be even possible, these are projects which only represent China's interests and do not take those of neighbouring states into consideration. Not everyone is on board with this, as the punitive tariffs upon China, imposed by the USA, demonstrate.

A further flaw in this strategy is China's decentralised political administrative organisation. When the central government in Beijing issues a directive, that does not mean that every province is willing to follow it. In many cases, the province would have a list of priorities which does not plan to allow for any changes. In the far north of China, living conditions are very different to those of the rich east. Despite the efforts of the government, the gap between the rich and the poor continues to grow. On the one side, people are unable to obtain fresh water; on the other side, some people are being given the newest watches from industrial mass production as gifts. Chinese investors pump millions into foreign companies but fail, due to language problems.

After many centuries of war, China has arrived where it has always wanted to be. The People's Republic is a superpower. The biggest army, the greatest industry, the largest population: China has all of that. However, the critical question that must be asked is how long this hard-earned upswing can last. In order to maintain the boom, the People's Republic must take care of the things which have been somewhat neglected in favour of the economy. Above all, this applies to human rights, transparency and real demographic facts, as China would never admit, that it does not really know its exact population figures.

Nevertheless, China is a super motor of the world's economy. This enables it to be significant on the world stage in such questions as climate change. China is presently an antagonist which believes itself to be in a special position. Its greatest aim is to generate prosperity through their economic achievements and it is constantly promising its people that it will prevail.

Because of the many existing international networks, today's global economy would be unthinkable without China. We would notice that not only but also on the cheap shoes available at present on the internet. We eat Chinese food items, use Chinese televisions and consume many other things that we do not even know about, which are made in the People's Republic. "Chinafication" is very noticeable in the Asian region.

China continues to grow at a speed which often makes those in the west catch their breath and shudder at the same time. Fears that the G-20 states should become a G-2 union are not so far-fetched. Of course, on paper this would never happen but the figures speak for themselves. China has long become number one in many branches. The only country to come close to them is the USA, although it is also beginning to falter in the face of the growth of the Chinese economy. The USA has allowed China to surpass it in many respects, and even though its own growth has been robust, China's growth has been faster and bigger. It remains to be seen if this trend is to continue. It will be interesting to see what happens when China becomes a fully industrialised country (experts predict this will be in 2050), with all its disadvantages, such as diseases of affluence and ageing problems. This will happen sometime, and then it will be seen how China reacts to the changing conditions.

Can China be considered a credible partner? Are the figures coming from the Chinese government - which does not even know the number of its own tax payers and could range in error by +/- 100 million inhabitants - really true? It can at least be assumed that the statistics vary according to the current party doctrine.

The Chinese continue to push forwards and it seems to be only a matter of time before we see whether it is a real boom or only a bubble which bursts when China runs out of the necessary resources to maintain its economy.

DID YOU ENJOY MY BOOK?

Now that you have read my book, you have had an in-depth look at Chinese culture. This is why I am asking you now for a small favour. Customer reviews are an important part of every product offered by Amazon. It is the first thing that customers look at and, more often than not, is the main reason whether or not they decide to buy the product. Considering the endless number of products available at Amazon, this factor is becoming increasingly important.

If you liked my book, I would be more than grateful if you could leave your review by Amazon. How do you do that? Just click on the "Write a customer review"-button (as shown below), which you find on the Amazon product page of my book or your orders site:

Review this product

Share your thoughts with other customers

> Write a customer review

Please write a short note explaining what you liked most and what you found to be most important. It will not take longer than a few minutes, promise!

Be assured, I will read every review personally. It will help me a lot to improve my books and to tailor them to your wishes.

For this I say to you:

Thank you very much!

Yours
Hermann

REFERENCES

Helwig Schmidt-Glintzer: Das neue China: von den Opiumkriegen bis heute. 6. Auflage. Beck, München 2014

Claudia Derichs, Thomas Heberer: Die politischen Systeme Ostasiens. 3. Auflage. Springer VS, Wiesbaden 2013

Thomas Scharping: Bevölkerungspolitik und demografische Entwicklung: Alte Probleme, neue Perspektiven. In: Doris Fischer (Hrsg.): Länderbericht China. Bundeszentrale für politische Bildung, 2014

China: wie ich es sehe, Erweiterte Neuauflage, 2. Auflage, von Krenz, Egon, 2019

The China Model: Political Meritocracy and the Limits of Democracy, von Bell, Daniel A, 2016

China: a history, von Bardoe, Cheryl, 2018

China: Situation und Perspektiven des neuen weltpolitischen Akteurs, von Benedikter, Roland, 2014

Vertagte Revolution: Die Politik der Kuomintang in China, 1923-1937, von Domes Jürgen, 2018

Politik in China: Beiträge zur Analyse chinesischer Politik, von Domes, Jürgen, hrsg. von Falter, Jürgen W. ¬[Hrsg.], 1992

Aspekte des sozialen Wandels in China: Familie, Bildung, Arbeit, Identität, hrsg. von Herrmann, Birgit Wieland, Eva Alpermann, Björn, 2018

Bildung und Berufsbildung in der Volksrepublik China: Strukturen, Probleme und Perspektiven, von Acuna, Christina, 2011

The Oxford companion to the economics of China, 1. Ausgabe, hrsg. von Fan, Shenggen, 2014

China - Wirtschaftsmacht der Zukunft, von Niembs, Martina, 1996

By all means necessary: how China's resource quest is changing the world, von Economy, Elizabeth C Levi, Michael A, 2014

Geschichte Chinas 1279-1949, von Dabringhaus Sabine, 2015

The Oxford illustrated history of modern China, First edition, unter Beteiligung von Wasserstrom, Jeffrey N. ¬[Herausgeber], 2016

China today, China tomorrow: domestic politics, economy, and society, unter Beteiligung von Fewsmith, Joseph, 2010

War, politics and society in early modern China, 900 – 1795, von Lorge, Peter Allan, 2005

Chinese politics: state, society and the market, hrsg. von Gries, Peter Hays ¬[Hrsg.] Rosen, Stanley ¬[Hrsg.], 2010

Chinesische Politik: nationale und globale Dimensionen, 2., aktualisierte und überarbeitete Auflage, von Noesselt, Nele, 2018

China regieren, 1. Aufl., von Xi, Jinping, 2014

Haus der Geschichte Bonn: www.hdg.de

Lexas Global History: www.globalhistory.de

Auswärtiges Amt: www.auswaertiges-amt.de

Bayerische Landesärztekammer:
https://www.blaek.de/

N-TV: www.ntv.de

Tagesspigel: www.tagespiegel.de

Deutschland-Portal: www.deutschland.de

Bundesministerium der Justiz und für
Verbraucherschutz: www.bmjv.de

Focus Online: www.focus.de

Campushunter: www.campushunter.de

Central Intelligence Agency:
https://www.cia.gov/library/publications/the-world-factbook/geos/us.html

LIPortal: www.liportal.de

Bundesministerium für Bildung und Forschung:
www.bmbf.de

Bundeszentrale für politische Bildung: www.bpb.de

Zeit online: www.Zeit.de

DISCLAIMER

Made in the USA
Las Vegas, NV
21 October 2020

10222590R00109